THE WRIGHT
E·X·I·T
STRATEGY

Wealth: How to Create It, Keep It and Use It

by
Bruce R. Wright

THE WRIGHT

E·X·I·T

STRATEGY

Wealth: How to Create It, Keep It and Use It

by
Bruce R. Wright

The Wright Company
Simi Valley, California
1-800-997-2664

Dedication

This book is dedicated to every person who is tired of the status quo and seeks a better way. Like many pioneers, my colleagues and I have taken a lot of arrows in mapping out this trail. May you have the courage and commitment to find and live a better way and to be a positive example and influence for others.

Acknowledgments

I owe a debt of gratitude to those who have helped to make this book possible, especially to Leanne Frost who met with me every week and "influenced" me into writing and rewriting on schedule. She and Sonja Bolle have also edited and re-edited, helped me clarify the messages, and helped with insight and perspective.

My friend and associate Mark Kastleman was always willing to be a sounding board and provided necessary doses of wisdom.

Thanks to my publisher and staff for their incessant pursuit and timely professionalism, as well as Joe Menkin who formatted the book, and the talented Jodie Williams who created the cartoons. Also to Mark Estes for his photography.

Noteworthy contributions of various kinds have been made by Jim Hollenbeck, Brad Barnes, Dan Cairns, Steve Takeda, Bill George, Thomas Quinlin, Joanne Johanson, Melinda Morris, and Peter Vedro.

This book would not have been possible without the love, patience and sacrifices of each of my family members. My lovely wife Jeanine has always supported me and tolerated my "outside the box" approach to life and business; she is truly "Mrs. Wright". Thank you Jeanine, Jason, Megan, Melissa, Jeremy, Jacob and Barry.

Most of all, thanks to those who read this book and recommend it to others, especially those advisors with the courage to pass it along to clients and prospective clients. It is a rare man or woman who risks a client relationship for such disclosure and insight.

Contents

SECTION I   WEALTH: HOW TO CREATE IT

Chapter 1   Wealth Principles   3
Chapter 2   Knowledge Can Be Power   15
Chapter 3   Appropriate Wealth Strategies   21

SECTION II   WEALTH: HOW TO KEEP IT

Chapter 4   If You Could Have the Perfect Situation:
            Planning to Achieve Your Goals   33
Chapter 5   Get In, Sit Down   37
Chapter 6   Seeing the Big Picture   49
Chapter 7   Your 100-Year Plan   53
Chapter 8   Where Are You Headed?   59
Chapter 9   Your Perfect Situation   63
Chapter 10   Financial Freedom   69
Chapter 11   Procrastination = Opportunity Lost   75
Chapter 12   Vision, Goals, Strategies, Tactics, Tools
            and Timing   79
Chapter 13   Micro Tactical Planning   87

SECTION III   WEALTH: HOW TO MANAGE IT
SELECTING ADVISORS

Chapter 14   Your All-Star Team   95
Chapter 15   Thinking, Doing and Being the Elephant:
            How Elephants Choose Advisors   109
Chapter 16   Crocodiles With a Smile   115
Chapter 17   Billy Bob, the One-Stop Shop   121
Chapter 18   Egomaniacs on the Loose   125
Chapter 19   The Good Ol' Boys and Girls   129
Chapter 20   Let Sleeping Dogs Lie   133
Chapter 21   Why Didn't You Tell Me About This When   137
Chapter 22   If They Could Have, Why Didn't They?   141
Chapter 23   Not Invented Here   145
Chapter 24   Show Me the Math   151

SECTION IV   WEALTH: HOW TO MANAGE IT
HOW TO AVOID BEING YOUR OWN WORST ENEMY

Chapter 25 Performing Surgery Without a Scalpel   157
Chapter 26 Severing the Ties   161
Chapter 27 It's Too Complicated   165
Chapter 28 But I Grew Up on That Property   173
Chapter 29 Putting on Your Overalls   177
Chapter 30 Analysis Paralysis   181
Chapter 31 Tough Love   185
Chapter 32 Price Versus Cost   191

SECTION V   WEALTH: HOW TO USE IT

Chapter 33 Creating, Living and Leaving a Legacy   201
Chapter 34 Children and Charity (First, Do No Harm)   207
Chapter 35 Sweet Charity: How to Choose or Create a
            Charity to Fulfill Your Legacy   211
Chapter 36 The Truth Will Set You Free   215

Preface

In order to progress or evolve as we go through life, we must expand our vision. Too often, people do not fully explore their opportunities and personal capabilities, or do not understand the full gravity of their existing or future problems. This book has been crafted to help people not only deal better with their money and their advisors, but to become better at life.

A couple of years ago, I had the privilege of meeting the author of the bestseller *The E Myth Revisited*, Michael Gerber, and his delightful wife, Ilene. Talking over lunch, I asked Michael if he could describe his business in 30 seconds or less. Always up to a challenge, Michael responded that he could do it if I could. And so the game began. Michael's response was brilliantly concise. He said, "We help small business owners get the business they've always wanted." His response to my query was astoundingly familiar.

When Michael challenged me to describe what my company, Estate & Foundation Services, Inc., did in 30 seconds or less, my response was, "We help people achieve the life they've always wanted, but usually didn't know they could have."

Having read Michael's books, I knew we shared common philosophies and had a similar appreciation of the universal truths of life, family and business. Since that meeting, we have had the pleasure of working together. On one occasion, we participated in a conference sponsored by a multinational investment firm directed at business owners and executives. The theme of the conference was "How to Get the Business and the Life You've Always Wanted.™"

When you think about it, loving one's work is important—even essential—to achieving happiness. But life should be about more than work and money. Most people have never *really* thought about defining their perfect life. It's not something we were taught to do. We weren't given the right tools. Michael's book is the best I've read for improving one's business—or, as Michael says, "Changing your job into a real business, one that is profitable without your having to work in it every day." His book offers ideas and processes that really work. It really can help small business owners get the businesses they have always wanted.

My book is about the bigger picture, about how to get from where you are today to a better life. The first section addresses proven methods for creating more wealth, concepts that have worked for me, my clients and many others. These are universal principles that can be applied regardless of where your true talents lie. Even if you believe you have accumulated enough wealth, please read the whole book. I promise that once you have read the entire book, you will see how the universal principles in the beginning hold their meaning throughout the book—and throughout your life. Please do not cheat yourself by skipping around, either.

Sections two, three and four of this book are dedicated to the principles of making the most of your wealth as it applies to real life—*your* life. You won't get bogged down in technical diatribes designed to impress you with my level of expertise. You will discover how to identify problems and opportunities, and gain insight on how to deal with them. You will learn more about how to select your advisors than many so-called advisors would like you to know.

The last section of this book will pull all of the components together to help you achieve a much improved quality of life, no matter how large or small your level of personal wealth.

This book contains all that is necessary for you to develop the ultimate exit strategy, a strategic plan to exit the things in your life that are driving you nuts or wasting your precious time, talents and resources. Since my companies and I have no involvement in the sale, promotion or profit-sharing from the sale of investments, insurance or annuities, you may rest assured that this book makes no attempt to "sell" you anything. I'm not trying to turn you into a client of my firm. In fact, if your existing advisors can work with you in the areas and processes outlined here, that would be great. I've applied the principles in this book not only to the lives of clients, but to my own life as well. It is time for me to move on—exit into—other things. I no longer wish to have as much involvement in strategic planning, macro or micro, for people. The principles I have taught and implemented have now been put on paper to benefit anyone who cares to discover them. The core elements of macro and micro strategic planning, thinking and doing are hereby available to everyone, irrespective of one's wealth, position, education or level of emotional or spiritual evolution. This book is primarily designed for the general public and as such contains all the principles the public needs.

Advisors who recommend this book to their existing or prospective clients are a rare breed. Only the most client-centered, proactive, truly professional advisors will distribute this book, because it defies the status quo of the industry. The principles contained in this book are perhaps even revolutionary. I didn't write this book to support the status quo; I wrote it to expose the truth. Eventually the truth will set you free. But only if you have the courage to look for it—then, once you have found it, to act upon it. I hope you will enjoy reading this book as much as I did writing it.

I

Wealth: How to Create It

1

Wealth Principles

Everywhere I go I hear people talking about how difficult it is in this day and age to generate wealth, to make one's fortune, to make one's mark in the world. This is utter nonsense; it is substantially easier today than it ever was in the past—if we can change our mindset and discover several truths about accumulating wealth.

The first step to creating wealth is to avoid buying into the myth that it is harder to create wealth today than it was before. That's not true; there are more millionaires per capita now than at any other time in history. Yet we are continually being told by the media and others how much more difficult it is today for people to buy homes, save for retirement, etc., because of higher interest rates; because of the tremendous tax burden we all share from the gasoline tax, property tax, garbage tax, school tax, city tax, state tax, federal tax, estate tax, etc.; because of the increased cost of living; and just the increased complexity of our time.

I was at a church gathering recently where this subject came up. The general consensus among the people in their 60s and older was that the younger generation has a much harder time establishing themselves for all the reasons listed above. But these churchgoers' perceptions were skewed by their past experiences, beliefs and paradigms. Many of these people were retired or about to retire. They were no longer actively looking for ways to create wealth. And, in many cases, because of the changes that have occurred over time, the specific ways in which they were accustomed to creating wealth in the past aren't as viable today. The older people speaking didn't see all of the opportunities around them, at least in part because they were no longer looking for opportunities.

If you talk to people who have recently achieved success or multimillion dollar status, the issue is not a lack of opportunity, but rather a bombardment of more opportunities than any one person can effectively deal with. Part of creating wealth is developing the ability to recognize opportunities. Once you do, they are virtually everywhere. Now, some opportunities are legitimate and can really help you achieve significant financial growth. However, some of these opportunities will only benefit people with certain talents and abilities and would not be valuable to others. We have to know what our talents and abilities are and recognize which opportunities are right for us and which opportunities are not.

This leads us to the next step: developing the power of discernment. While surfing the television channels, you will inevitably come across a "How to Get Rich Quick" infomercial. The spokesperson will be saying, "This is an opportunity that comes along only once in your lifetime, and this may be the only opportunity you ever have to get rich." The challenge today in terms of creating personal wealth is to develop a power of discernment, an ability to recognize your own strengths and weaknesses, and go for the opportunities that suit you. Don't believe that just because an opportunity presents itself it is your only chance; it may or may not be right for you, but it certainly won't be the only opportunity to come along.

When developing the power of discernment, we should not let our past experiences limit us by saying, "Gee, I wasn't successful at such-and-such when I tried it, so therefore I won't be able to succeed at this new thing." I once had a business partner who never wanted to try anything new. Every time I had an idea about how to innovate the business, generate additional revenue and create more equity for the partners in that firm, his response was, "There you go again. Listen, this is 1984, and there are no new ideas. Every idea you have has already been thought up before." If you believed this, then you would have to believe there could never be another new song because virtually every note that could possibly be heard has already been played, and every word that could be written about love, feelings or passion has already been sung.

It's astounding that there are so many people who are willing to believe that nothing new can ever be thought up or done. In the late 1800s, the head of the U.S. Patent Office basically said that anything and everything that ever needed to be invented or could be invented had already been invented. Imagine his surprise today. Anyone who tells you there's no such thing as a new idea is a member of what I call the "square wheel tribe." Here's what they look like:

The square wheel tribe, working diligently

The guys pushing the cart think they are really doing well; they're making progress, aren't they? Their cart with square wheels is moving their load much more efficiently than if they had to carry the cargo on their backs, which is what they did before they became really innovative and invented this cart with square wheels. These guys believe they've really developed the ultimate in transportation: this cart with square wheels. If you were to approach these people and say, "Hey, I have an idea for you. What if you stopped for just a minute and took the square wheels off and put the round wheels on? I think you'd be much more efficient, you'd make a lot more progress, and your business would be more profitable," the people of the square wheel tribe would refuse your suggestion and argue with you.

They would say, "Who do you think you are? We invented the cart with the square wheels. We are the ones who innovated the market. We are the ones who created this drastically superior method of transporting cargo. Who are you to tell us anything? I mean, these round things we're transporting were thought up by some looney-tune start-up company. It's never going to catch on, and frankly, we're making money off of these morons by charging them to transport their stupid round wheels. These guys are going to be a flash in the pan. They're going to be gone in no time. There are no ideas as good as the idea we had seven years ago when we created this wonderfully efficient vehicle you see before you. We are the market leader. We are the innovator, and everything that needs to be done with regard to transportation has already been done. And we, my friend, are the ones who have done it."

Part of creating wealth is to avoid becoming a member of the square wheel tribe. Dr. Stephen R. Covey, author of *The Seven Habits of Highly Effective People*, explained it well when he said the leader is the one who climbs the tallest tree, surveys the entire situation, and yells, "Wrong jungle." But what do the busy, efficient managers and workers say? "Shut up, we're making progress." I would not only echo Dr. Covey's words, but I would add this thought: Sometimes good can be the enemy of great.

If you're struggling, you'll be looking harder for opportunities to change and get ahead. If you're doing just fine, you tend to become complacent and perhaps miss out on opportunities to become great. Although a lot of ideas have already been thought up by somebody else, a lot of us have thought of ideas that would make things better. When I started mountain biking aggressively and regularly, I started thinking, "Boy, it would be nice if there were more places to put my hands on the handlebars. I sure get tired of putting my hands in the same place all the time." I started talking to my friends about how it would be neat if the bar was longer and curved around the front, or if there was a little secondary bar that stuck out and that you could grab onto when you were climbing hills or just riding on flat, easy terrain when you didn't have to have your hands on your brakes. My friends of the square wheel persuasion said, "That's a dumb idea." Then, not more than a year and a half later, handlebar add-ons, or bar-ends as you'd call them today, are all the rage. It's very hard to find a quality mountain bike now that doesn't have an extra piece for the handlebars so that you can have multiple hand positions.

There are all kinds of good ideas out there. The people who invented the round wheels, which our square-wheeled friends are pushing, set themselves apart from all the other people in the world who may have thought of the possibility of round wheels by actually doing something about it. They went out and built the round wheels. They innovated and improved upon someone else's idea. Somebody will come along and say, "It might be a good idea if we put brakes on these wheels. When we had the square wheels, we didn't have to worry about the cart taking off down a hill, but with these round wheels, we need some type of braking mechanism to stop the cart from getting away from us, or worse, running over us." Somebody else will take a look at the situation down the road and say, "If we make this cart out of something lighter than wood, we could carry more cargo; therefore, we'd make more money with each trip. Our payload would increase." Then, somebody else will come along and say, "Maybe instead of having people push and pull this thing, we should attach horses to it." And then someone else will come along and attach a motor to it, and somebody else will improve upon that. Eventually the cart will be made out of some space-age titanium boron material originally thought up by the defense industry and applied to this transportation vehicle, and it will hover rather than use wheels at all. There's no end to where the innovation can go.

Part of creating wealth is looking for innovation. What can you improve upon? How can you make things better? How can you improve the world? How can you improve relationships? How can you improve mechanical or electronic technology? When you really begin to look for ways to create wealth, you will find a never-ending stream of opportunities. Many are produced or published as infomercials, advertisements, classifieds in the back of magazines, books, tapes or videos. There are all kinds of ways to "get rich quick."

Although it's not my intention to disparage any of those products—because nearly all of them will work for somebody—a lot of people who devise these courses and manuals have never been very successful themselves. Some of them are just good at getting other people to try it, and there are enough talented people out there that they'll get some success stories. I think you have to guard against those types of so-called opportunities. If you were to acquire all of those products and evaluate them and then try to apply them, you might find that some of them would work for you and could generate substantial amounts of equity or net worth.

However, you would also probably find that many of them couldn't work for you. Some couldn't work for anyone.

Although there are many ways in which you can create wealth, the key to successfully evaluating your opportunities is to develop your power of discernment. There are so many "quick" but not worthwhile methods being touted because the one thing that has remained consistent over thousands of years is human nature. Human nature is still the same today as it was a thousand, two thousand or three thousand years ago. People are still inclined to take the path of least resistance. Those who are able to rise above their natural inclinations tend to succeed in many areas of their lives. Their success, their ability to create a substantial amount of net worth, by and large stems from their ability to avoid certain traps of human nature such as laziness, selfishness and complacency. They shun the path of least resistance.

For example, meet the Green family. Although that's not their real name, this is their true story. Many years ago Grandpa Green worked for an electrical power company. This was back in the days when electricity was new. There weren't any dominant electric companies in the country yet; electrical power wasn't even available in the more rural areas. Grandpa Green did his job, working every day to earn money to support his wife and kids. And although he always did his job, the company wasn't always as profitable as they'd have liked to be, and they weren't always able to make payroll, at least not the whole payroll. The first time this happened, the company called Grandpa Green into their offices and said, "You're a good, hard worker, and what we'd like to do is to give you some stock in our company in lieu of compensation because we're having a cash flow problem right now."

Grandpa Green wasn't interested in stock in the company, particularly stock in a company that couldn't make its payroll. But, on the other hand, there was this thing called the Depression going on, so he didn't really have much choice but to accept their offer. It wasn't as if he could just go take his pick of 20 other jobs. He was fortunate to have any income at all. He took the stock and lived with it.

This happened often enough over a period of time that he acquired a fair amount of stock in this fledgling company. He continued to work for the company, and by the time he died, he had quite a bit of stock. Being a hard-working, American-values, traditional kind of fellow, he didn't spend much of anything. He saved his money. He lived within his means. He certainly wasn't about to go out and liquidate the stock, because after all, he was able to get by with what income he had, and most of the stock was acquired during the leaner, earlier years. The company had been able to pay him pretty well later on. He really didn't have any reason to sell the stock.

When Grandpa Green died, he left an equal amount of stock to each of his three daughters and some of the stock to each of his four grandchildren. The four grandchildren, three sisters and one brother, each got an equal share. The grandson, Frank, was very much like his grandfather. He lived within his means. He loved his job coaching baseball. It did not pay very much but was satisfying in every other respect. Frank and his wife, Joan, kept virtually all of their stock.

Frank's sisters, on the other hand, married people who, like themselves, had a tendency to spend money. And so over time, the three sisters liquidated their stock because they wanted to have bigger houses, ski boats, snowmobiles and new cars every few years. They always needed something. So they found many, many "reasons" why they had to liquidate the stock.

When I met the grandson, Frank, he was 55 years old. He had coached his whole life. His sisters viewed him as a financial failure. Frank didn't conform to the idea of what the family thought he should be doing with his money because he had held onto his grandpa's stock. Now the stock had a completely different name than when his grandfather initially got it because the grandfather's company had been absorbed by a bigger company, and that was absorbed by another bigger company, and so on and so forth, and Frank now owned $4 million of General Electric stock in the middle of the biggest bull market in the history of the world. Within nine months, Frank's stock rose in value to $5.5 million.

So, here were Frank and Joan with $5.5 million of General Electric stock. Two of his three sisters could measure their net worth in a few hundred thousand dollars each, and most of that was in their husbands' retirement funds. The third sister's net worth was close to zero because she had taken out second and third mortgages on her home. Frank's sisters had given in to human nature. Frank resisted his natural tendencies, lived within his means, went without the luxuries his sisters felt they needed, and came out ahead in the end.

Sacrifice is part of creating wealth. I was watching a television program on PBS not too long ago called *Revenge of the Nerds*—not the movie, but a documentary. The host of the show was talking about Microsoft and how it got started in a small house in the Bay Area. He was part of the original group who worked and lived in that house. They were sleeping in sleeping bags on the floor, working crazy hours, playing loud rock music and living on Coca-Cola, pizza and peanut butter sandwiches. Instead of staying with Bill Gates and his upstart company, the host of the show said he listened to the people around him who said he was crazy working for this little company that couldn't even afford office space. They encouraged him to get a real job. Shortly thereafter, he quit.

There are people who walk away from tremendous opportunities simply because they lack the vision or the belief in whatever it is they are doing, or are unwilling to sacrifice now for success later. They follow the path of least resistance, the path of conformity. Sometimes you have to think of opportunity as an old well, where you have to prime the pump. You're pumping and pumping and pumping, and nothing is coming out. You're working hard and sweating, and after a while you just give up and leave. But at that moment, the water is only three inches from the spout, about to burst forth. Since you didn't know that, you stopped, and the water went all the way back down into the well again. History has proven that enduring to the end is a principle of success.

How many people miss out on opportunities? How many people missed out on the Microsoft opportunity simply because they didn't stick with it? They didn't have the vision; they didn't believe in themselves; they didn't believe in the people around them. Or maybe they didn't understand the concept of sacrifice: In order to get what I really want in the long run, I have to give up something I really want today.

Unfortunately, we have ample proof around us of how many people disregard the principle of sacrifice. We have, for example, all the quick weight-loss programs that say, "Just take this drug, and you'll be thin; you can still eat anything you want to." Losing weight by taking in fewer calories and exercising more is just too much work. The path of least resistance is to take the drug or drink the miracle shake. People are always looking for some shortcut because it's easier than sacrificing and working hard.

If I'd really like to have the body of a professional bodybuilder, but I really want to eat these chocolates, hmmm, what am I going to do? I could eat these chocolates and take this magic pill and believe that I'm going to look like a bodybuilder. How many people find out after going to the gym and diligently working out for months that they're not going to look like a world-famous bodybuilder, so they start taking drugs like steroids in order to increase their muscle mass and definition?

These are the kinds of things that people do all the time, and of course, the do-it-quick-and-easy methods are all multibillion-dollar industries. These industries are built upon one of the primary negative aspects of human nature, which is the tendency to pursue the path of least resistance. In fact, throughout the course of this book I will cite numerous examples of how taking the path of least resistance almost always leads to failure to obtain the truly desirable end result. The bodybuilders take the steroids and get the great bodies, but internally their organs are all shot and they're dying.

If you are prone to pursue the path of least resistance, if you are prone to believe that you can, for $29.95 or $195, buy some course, book or series of tapes and you're going to become wealthy because you purchased that stuff, it's time to wake up and understand that it doesn't work that way. If you are going to succeed with any system, you're going to have to work at it. And you're going to have to sacrifice something that you would rather do in order to achieve that more desirable result.

Another very important principle of creating wealth is to live within your means and make sure you are working toward some specific goals for the future. I suspect you won't see me as a spokesperson for a credit card company because what I'm really promoting here is the idea of abstinence. Abstain from spending money that you don't really have or can't really afford to spend. On the other hand, I would suggest that you can't make money without spending money either. So, again, you have to develop the power of discernment to wisely decide how, when, where and on what to spend your money.

You also need to learn how to spend your *time* wisely. How you develop your talents and abilities is critical to creating wealth. It doesn't really make any difference whether you make your money by purchasing real estate for "no money down" from person A or B's course, selling something on the Internet, running classified ads, developing an idea and turning it into an actual business or buying an existing business. All of these are viable means to the end of obtaining wealth. It is more important to grasp the concept of what creating wealth is all about.

Succinctly put, to gain wealth you must develop your talents and abilities, look for opportunities to maximize your abilities, work hard and avoid obstacles that may impede your opportunities for success. In this chapter we've discussed several ways to avoid the roadblocks to success, including:

- Don't accept the myth that it is harder to make money now than before.

- Avoid becoming a member of or associating with the "square wheel tribe."

- Look for innovation.

- Develop your power of discernment.

- Resist giving in to human tendencies to be complacent or to take the path of least resistance.

- Be willing to sacrifice something now for greater success later.

- Live within your means.

- Learn to spend your time wisely and develop your talents and abilities.

Never forget the immortal words of Alan Kay, futurist, innovator and author, "The best way to predict your future is to create it."

The following personal story was pulled from the *Inc.* magazine of October, 1997. After reading this passage, I hope you will see why *Inc.* is a must read for anyone who wants to succeed in business:

> For years my role as the wife of a professional speaker was to sit in the last row of an auditorium and shout, 'Louder!' whenever my husband's voice dropped. I decided that there had to be a better feedback device, and if there wasn't, I was going to in-

vent one. Then I decided, at the age of 80-plus, that I would start a business to sell it.

My children thought I'd gone off my rocker. Friends were more tactful, but I resented their sometimes patronizing comments. ('Marvelous that you can still do it!') Of course, the reactions weren't surprising. Though start-ups have become our national pastime, they're considered a young person's game—certainly not an appropriate activity for senior citizens.

But starting a business at 80 is really no different from starting one at any age. The only prerequisites are that you are still alive, in good physical and mental health, and the owner of a vast reservoir of energy. One's sense of urgency is a plus: if not now, when?

Please pay special attention to the last sentence from the first paragraph of the quote. "Then I decided, at the age of 80-plus, that I would start a business to sell it." The writer is not planning just to sell the feedback device; she is talking about selling the enterprise. This is a crucial concept, and one I shall devote a lot of coverage to. If you start or buy a business, make sure you have a mindset that includes selling it. Those who fail to include an "exit strategy" in their plans are in danger of becoming slaves to their career, job or business.

The next step is to capitalize on your wealth-creating abilities.

2

Knowledge Can Be Power

For a long time the widely held belief has been, "Knowledge is power." Those who have achieved high levels of success have added, "Knowledge combined with action is power." However, because of rapidly developing technology and the high-speed, persistent change of our day, these statements must be expanded even further. Knowledge without imagination cannot evolve. Imagination is the lifeblood of creativity, the mother of innovation and knowledge. Those who choose to succeed must embrace and live by this new paradigm and credo: "Constantly evolving knowledge combined with innovative action is power."

If you want to get ahead of the pack and acquire your desired amount of wealth or financial independence while you are young and/or healthy enough to enjoy it, you should turbocharge your brain. You should strive to increase your business acumen constantly. That means to perform an adequate amount of timely research and to read a lot about business. I recommend you divide your wealth-building reading or education program into the following categories and percentages:

1. Existing or desired business field—35%

2. Semi-related or unrelated business fields—20%

3. Spiritual development—20%

4. Human relationships/personal development—20%

5. Hobbies/enjoyment—5%

Many significant breakthroughs come when we are not looking for them. By balancing our continuing education habits, we simultaneously balance our lives. When learning about issues seemingly unrelated to my core business, I often "accidentally" discover universal truths and figure out how to tie them into my core business, improve my personal skills such as parenting, or generally become more effective in life and relationships. This increase in knowledge and perspective makes me more valuable to my clients. With a balanced research or education program, answers to difficult problems are found. Our breadth of perception is dramatically increased. As our breadth of perception improves, our ability to improve in technical competency almost magically reaches higher and better levels.

A well balanced education program equals a well balanced person. If you seek out the wisest people on earth, you will find them to be committed to ongoing balanced education. There are no "secrets to success." Everything you need to succeed is readily available if you will just work at it. Turbocharge your brain by putting your life in balance. Once on this path, you will discover how to turbocharge your business and your ability to attract opportunities and wealth. You can become a magnet for wealth and opportunity. The power of discernment will become critical to the sorting process, the selection of what opportunities are best for you at a given time in your life and level of skill.

Some people find that a balanced education program is impractical if it is to be implemented only through reading. Personally, I find books on tape to be a tremendous advantage. Over the years, I have amassed quite a library of audio books. During most months, I "hear" two or three books and read 12-15 magazines on a variety of topics. I have never met anyone who could not also benefit by studying the scriptures or otherwise increasing their spiritual evolution.

Success ultimately comes to those who implement a series of correct principles. Over the years, I have written quite a few business innovation plans for financial services professionals as well as strategic plans for wealthy individuals and their families. Those who have implemented parts of the plans have enjoyed varying degrees of improvement. Most important, those who have implemented their plans as intended, or completely, have experienced quantum improvements in their lives and/or their finances and businesses. A common mistake many people make is that they fail to implement each and every element needed to succeed. For example, if a strategic plan for an individual contains 10 items, he or she should implement each item on or before the deadline given. Far too many people treat their action list as if it were a menu. They choose those components which will be the easiest or tastiest and skip many of the essential but less attractive items.

When you lead thirsty horses to water, they will usually drink. One of our company mottos is, "Spend your time, talent and resources only with the thirsty horses." They are most likely to implement all of the steps necessary to take them where they want to go. You can look at it like the Constitution of the United States. All of the parts go together. If you leave out or ignore the first, second and fourth amendments to the Constitution, eventually the whole thing will erode into nothingness. If you want to keep your freedom, uphold the entire Constitution, not just the "easy" or most likeable or "politically correct" parts. Most religions that teach the Ten Commandments also teach that you should follow all of them. If you believe in heaven and you want to get there, follow all of the Ten Commandments. If you want to succeed in business and/or enjoy a more fulfilling life, implement all of the proven principles and components which lead to success. It will not be easy. Sometimes your journey will be boring, tiresome, perhaps even frightening and treacherous. You must be willing to keep on working at it when most "normal" people will already have quit.

Adversity

Nothing really worth having is easily obtained. That which is too easily obtained will be little valued. These are a couple of universal principles which life constantly brings to our attention. Adversity in the right doses is a beneficial thing. Remember the saying, "That which doesn't kill us only makes us stronger." A person's ability to deal with adversity can be improved because adversity management is a skill rather than a talent. Not everyone who wants to be a professional athlete or musician has the necessary level of talent and, thus, cannot develop the high level of skills to realize that dream. Adversity management is a completely different game. In fact, talent has little to do with managing adversity. All one has to do is master the appropriate skills and techniques.

One of my favorite books on tape is *Adversity Quotient: Turning Obstacles Into Opportunities* by Paul G. Stoltz, Ph.D. This book is really "outside the box" and is exactly on target. Dr. Stoltz uses a mountain-climbing metaphor to teach us how to overcome and even profit by adversity. Dr. Stoltz teaches that the mountain represents our purpose in life or in business. All people will enjoy their greatest success and fulfillment by relentlessly pursuing their purpose or mission, and we each determine the mental paradigm or mindset with which we approach our personal mountains. Dr. Stoltz breaks the paradigms down into three key types:

- **Quitters**—These are people who abandon the climb when things get tough. They have little tolerance for adversity. They quickly lose the will to climb and think only about survival. They lose sight of their real purpose or mission or have never had a sense of purpose in their lives.

- **Campers**—These people have some ambition and a little more tolerance for pain than quitters. Another way to describe them is "complacent." Once a certain level of comfort is reached, they decide to take it easy. "We'll camp right here," they say. "This may not be all we hoped for, but it is pretty good." These are the most likely people to join the square wheel tribe. Improvement, let alone innovation, comes at a price they are generally unwilling to pay.

- **Climbers**—These people are willing to keep on trying even long after it begins to hurt. These people have a long-term vision of reaching the top of their mountain. Rather than quitting or camping in the face of adversity, climbers innovate. They try new ideas or new approaches. They just "know" there is a way to get around every obstacle. If they can't find a way to climb the mountain, they will build a helicopter and fly to the top. Climbers constantly pursue excellence in themselves and encourage it in those around them.

I hope Dr. Stoltz doesn't mind my broad interpretation of his writings. Should you take the time and effort to read or listen to his book, you will benefit by his systematic approach to mastering adversity.

With the exception of some who have inherited their wealth, every wealthy person I've met chose to be a climber. The great thing about this philosophy is that it applies to anyone who wants to succeed. Regardless of your race, background, environment, religion, childhood, parents or physical challenges, you can learn the skills to master adversity. You are where you are comfortable. It's all up to you!

3

Appropriate Wealth Strategies

Throughout the last 10 years or so of my career, virtually all of my clients have been very successful people by anyone's standards. And even though they have all created their own wealth in various ways, they all have one flaw in common—they didn't have a personal strategic plan that included entrance, growth and exit strategies. The idea was, "Let's make a lot of money," but they didn't really have specific goals. For example, they didn't really think about how much was going to be enough. If you don't articulate how much is enough, you tend to work much longer than you need to. In other words, you'll end up acquiring substantially more wealth than you can personally benefit from or even than your heirs can personally benefit from.

Anyone who is looking to become successful could learn from some clients of mine named John and Sharon. They met when they were young, fell in love and got married. John went to work for a very large telecommunications company where he supervised 1200 people. An opportunity presented itself for him to become involved in a start-up enterprise. After he thought long and hard about it and endured many sleepless nights, he overcame his initial fear of the uncertainty the opportunity brought with it, and he went for it. John became the CEO of a small high-tech company in Silicon Valley. He took the company public and built it up to several hundred employees and worldwide distribution.

Like many companies, it went through the growth phase of the business cycle, moving from being a small, new company with uncertain prospects to being a valuable entity. Its stock reached $32 a share, and the future looked pretty bright. However, John knew that in the typical business cycle, once the height of the growth curve is reached, it is usually downhill from there. So, instead of becoming complacent, John began looking for opportunities to prolong or even increase the company's growth and avoid a downward trend.

One day he was introduced to two men who had entered the government lottery to win a permit to operate telecommunications satellites. By pure luck, they won one of the permits; they now had the right to launch two satellites. What they didn't have was very much business experience, personal connections or capital. But they were persistent and hard working, and they weren't going to give up.

John was extremely well connected within the telecommunications industry and devised a way to enter into a joint venture with these two men so they could all benefit from their permit. The idea was that they could then enter other strategic alliances and create an entirely new division for the company that would innovate the business and move it to the next level. Unfortunately, many members of the square wheel tribe sat on John's board. They had already outvoted him on some other key issues, and they decided, "We're not going to do this."

For John, this was the straw that broke the camel's back. He decided he had the contacts to arrange the joint venture himself, preserve the satellite permit and maybe even create a very profitable new business. In fact, it had the potential to be considerably more successful than the existing company. So John obtained his board's permission to make the deal on his own and resigned from the company.

In a few weeks John managed to assemble the strategic alliance members and put together a series of contracts to make the deal happen. In the process, he was able to create a substantial amount of wealth for himself and each of the original permit owners.

John and Sharon, in the midst of all this, began to realize they needed to learn more about structuring their finances. Their research eventually led them to my company. We started our meeting off with the normal pleasantries. John outlined his business history and said, "Now we've got a multimillion dollar income and a horrendous tax situation, as well as other difficult issues to plan for. We're not sure exactly what to do. We've been talking to our other lawyers and accountants, but they're not telling us anything we can really agree to or fully understand. We want to get your opinion."

The first question I asked was, "John, when you were getting together to form this business relationship with the permit holders, what was the real agenda for the meeting?"

He said, "We brought our respective attorneys and accountants together to decide what type of business we were going to form: a limited liability company, limited partnership, general partnership, S corporation or C corporation. We also wanted to decide who would own how much of the company, how many shares would be issued, how many shares would be outstanding, and those kinds of typical things."

"I see," I said. "But, what was the real purpose of the meeting?"

He looked at me as if to say, "Are you deaf? I just covered that." And he slowly answered, "Well, as I just said, the purpose of the meeting was to determine what type of business entity we were going to create and how the ownership was going to be divided."

"I think it's important to become clear as to what the real purpose of that meeting was," I insisted. "Why did you get together?"

Before John could say anything, his wife slugged him in the arm, and said, "John, you went to the meeting because you wanted to make money."

John said, "Well, that goes without saying."

I said, "Well, obviously it went without saying because nobody said it."

"I don't think I understand what you mean," John said.

I continued, "Let me see if I've got this right. At the time, your business enterprise owned a permit to launch two satellites. One would provide telecommunications, television, etc., coverage throughout South America; the second would be launched later to provide telecommunications coverage from basically Chicago westward throughout about half of Asia."

"Correct," John said.

"Did anyone in this meeting think this business opportunity was going to be profitable?" I asked.

Becoming visibly irritated, John said, "Well, if we didn't think it was going to be profitable, we wouldn't have been doing it."

"It's just curious," I said. "It doesn't seem as though anyone really thought it was going to be profitable, because now you've got all these millions of dollars in taxes that have to be paid. I just can't help but wonder why, if you and your partners all believed it was going to be successful and you were all going to generate millions of dollars of personal net worth, you didn't choose to form this enterprise and take title in such a way that you would be able to retain as much equity, value, revenue, etc., on a net-after-tax basis as possible?"

There was a pregnant pause. And then John said, "I guess we just kind of dropped the ball on that."

Here had been a wonderful business opportunity. Everyone was convinced it was going to work and be very profitable. And it was. However, their approach had three primary flaws:

1. No suitable entrance strategy for the business.

2. No *personal* growth or wealth accumulation strategy for the owners.

3. No effective exit strategy for the owners.

What was needed was a macro strategic plan, which would include the following elements:

The Entrance Strategy

Instead of hoping that professionals would help them fix their current problems, John and his partners should have developed a suitable entrance strategy. This is a preeminent problem in the wealth creation process. I would say 99.5% of the people who create these multimillion or multibillion dollar companies don't have an entrance strategy designed to protect personal wealth. They create wonderfully profitable businesses, but not enough of the wealth comes to them personally in tax-advantaged and efficiently distributed ways. Tremendous amounts of otherwise avoidable taxes and other expenses and fees are lost simply because people don't go into a venture properly structured, even though they are confident it is going to succeed. Every successful business person I've worked with understands the importance and value of a sound strategic business plan for their enterprise. It's just amazing, however, that they don't simultaneously create a personal strategic plan in order to assure sound vision and focus.

The Growth Strategy

Typically when people create a business enterprise, they believe it's going to succeed, and they focus on building a profitable business. Sometimes they are able to do so. The business grows; it becomes very valuable. But unfortunately, it doesn't always transfer to them personally. They have a growth strategy for the business, but they don't have a clearly articulated growth or accumulation strategy for themselves. If they did, they would hold title to their assets differently at the beginning of the growth phase than they commonly do.

The Exit Strategy

The third element that must be addressed is an effective exit strategy. I'm not talking about retiring from the business enterprise; I'm talking about a strategy for moving out of the business. In other words, first you must determine how much is enough. How much money do you really need to enjoy financial freedom? Second, you have to realize when you have enough. We ask our clients to answer the question, "If you could have the perfect situation, what would it be?" Take a look at your current calendar. Is it filled with meetings, appointments, responsibilities and activities that you would rather not be doing? When you reach the point where you actually have all the wealth you need, wouldn't it make sense to exchange your current calendar for your perfect calendar, a calendar that is filled with what you would really like to be doing? In essence, if you need $10 million of personal net worth to be happy, fulfilled and free to pursue the best use of your time, talent and resources, then the real issue is: When do you get there? If you can get there in one business deal, as in John's case, or in five years or ten years, or whatever the time frame happens to be, if you can in fact get there, you need to recognize when you are actually there. And when it happens, you need to get out of the old calendar and exit into the perfect or at least better calendar.

At my firm, we typically see people who are very successful at obtaining very substantial amounts of wealth. They have created millions of dollars, tens of millions, sometimes hundreds of millions of dollars of personal net worth, but they're not living the perfect calendar. Their calendars are full of things they'd rather not be doing. But, maybe just through habit, they're caught up in it, or maybe they just don't have a clear mindset, strategy, vision or understanding of tactics and timing to exit. An effective exit strategy answers the questions:

- How much is enough?
- When is it enough?
- What are my tactics going to be to get out of calendar A and into calendar B?

These are critical issues that are ignored and/or not appropriately addressed by financial services professionals or by the consumers of their services. Some of these people are very good at creating profitable business enterprises, but they overlook the people part of the issue. It should all be about the people. Why would anybody go through all the sacrifices, headaches, stress and difficulties that are necessary parts of becoming wealthy, if they aren't personally going to benefit from it? I believe the people creating the wealth are more important than the wealth itself.

If you're thinking about creating wealth or have already done so, you need to ask yourself, "Why am I creating this wealth?" If your paradigm is, "I'm going to create a successful company," that's wonderful. But how does that benefit you personally? Having successfully created wealth once, people tend to be much more aware of these issues on the second or third go around.

Our client Barry is great at starting companies and building them up to a value of about $100 million. Barry built one company as CEO, took it public, and then realized he no longer really fit into that enterprise. So he got out to go on to the next thing. His primary interest, talents and strengths revolve around the creation of new enterprises and turning them into something valuable. That's something he loves to do. His strengths don't lie in the area of maintaining and running a company in the other phases. So he exited; he got out. But he didn't have a personal entrance, growth and exit strategy, so he got hammered on taxes. He lost approximately 40% of the equity he had accumulated over several years because he was ill prepared for the success he would eventually achieve.

When I met Barry, he was getting ready to exit from his second business venture, and he had learned from his previous experience. Instead of just trying to "make money," he had set some specific goals. He had decided to exit when his stock reached $20 a share. And as part of his entrance strategy, he had decided to not keep all of the wealth in his and his wife's name—partially for tax purposes, but also to achieve some of his other goals. He had decided to create some wealth for his two daughters so that they would be financially independent; however, he wanted to control their access to the money and how it was invested. So his entrance strategy included the implementation of a trust mechanism, partnership, and a series of tactics to give him the control he wanted, but to pass his wealth to his daughters as effectively as possible without losing a large portion to taxes when his company succeeded.

His growth strategy certainly worked, and he gave shares of stock to his two daughters at $1 a share using his and his wife's $10,000 annual gifts. The stock was now worth $22 a share. His daughters each had more than $2 million of that stock, and by implementing some specific tactics that were available at the time, we were able to utilize tax-advantaged trusts, liquidate a significant portion of the family's and/or their trusts' holdings in this stock and get them out at $22 a share without their having to pay capital gains tax. It literally saved them millions of dollars in taxes.

Most of the people we meet wish they had done what Barry did. But they didn't because they never got around to it, they were too busy, or they just didn't know how to do it. They didn't have the knowledge even though they often had corporate legal counsel, accountants, CFOs and other advisors. Barry originally planned on implementing his exit strategy and tactics with a typical "full service" financial services firm; however, after a brief telephone conversation we had, Barry realized the financial services firm was not going to provide him with the level of objective, third-party advice and information he wanted. So he opted to work with us.

Barry used his exit strategy to make the most of what he had built. Bill, his good friend and senior vice president of marketing for his company, didn't. Barry and Bill were both thinking about exiting the company while the stock was trading at just above $22 a share. The problem was that Bill didn't have an exit strategy. Bill had never made millions of dollars before; this was his first time through the process. He didn't have an entrance strategy, a growth strategy or an exit strategy. Instead he thought, "I'm going to get a job, and I'll get some stock in the company. Hopefully, someday it will be worth a lot of money."

His hope came true, but because he lacked a real strategy, he didn't have a disciplined approach to managing his affairs. His excuse was that he was too busy. He was in charge of worldwide sales and was so busy doing his job that he didn't think about its real value and the impact on him personally. If he had taken the time to formulate a plan, he would have realized that $16 a share was his "magic number." At $16 a share, he would have reached financial freedom.

Even though the stock at one point was worth $22, within a couple of months the stock value declined to approximately $8 a share. Barry was already out of the stock, but for Bill, this was devastating. At $8 a share, Bill only had half the net worth he needed to execute his exit strategy. Bill still had to work.

Like Bill, we need to realize when we become a multimillion-dollar enterprise. Bill should have said, "My first and foremost responsibility is that of CEO of Bill Enterprises." As CEO of yourself, you can't manage every single aspect of your life. You need to get a support team. You need division managers, a team of expert advisors to help you.

Barry and Bill have subsequently entered another business venture together. Barry doesn't need to make a dime on this next business venture in order to be financially free and live happily ever after, but Bill is tremendously dependent upon the success of this next venture. It really needs to succeed in order for him to be able to exit. Bill's stress level is considerably greater than Barry's, for obvious reasons.

By objectively reviewing Bill's situation, we can identify several obstacles to creating wealth that could have been avoided:

- Bill didn't have a personal entrance, growth or exit strategy. Therefore, he had no "magic number." He didn't know how much was enough.

- Bill wasn't disciplined. He didn't realize *when* enough was enough. He didn't have a team of financial professionals, a SWAT team of highly competent people, to help oversee his financial situation. When he was busy doing his job, there was nobody watching Bill's personal financial enterprise.

- Bill was busy creating tremendous value for the business but did not understand the reason why he was working. He did not realize that his primary objective should have been creating wealth to obtain his personal financial freedom.

Part of creating wealth is determining what your personal entrance, growth and exit strategies are. There are thousands of books on how to start and run businesses, how to make them effective, and how to deal with the various business cycles. Besides books, there are numerous tapes, videos, training programs, consultants, etc. Taking all the information available and applying it to your personal strategies occurs in the three following phases.

Phase One: Gaining a true desire to create enough wealth so that the wealth supports you; then you no longer have to work for your own sustenance. You are committed to the concept of financial independence, reaching financial freedom. Include this in your personal mission statement and in your entrance strategies for various career moves, business start-ups, acquisitions, etc.

Phase Two: Researching and developing how you're going to get from where you are now to your "magic number." Create a written plan to achieve your objectives.

Phase Three: Writing your objectives down on paper and having the discipline to execute your exit strategy at the appropriate time. Don't make the mistake Bill made. If you're financially independent in April, and then in August you've lost half your net worth through no fault of your own except a lack of diligence, you can't blame anybody but yourself.

A key point here is that an exit strategy isn't about getting out of anything you love to do. There are some people who love the work they do. I was talking with one of my clients recently who knows one of the wealthiest men in the world. He said, "What's with this guy? He's worth billions of dollars, and he's still working."

I said, "He's not working, though. He does it because he loves it." If he is living the perfect calendar, then it isn't work. It's what he loves to do.

It's all about living the perfect calendar. The exit strategy doesn't have anything to do with giving up what you love to do if, in fact, you believe that what you're doing is really the best use of your time, talent and resources. However, sometimes because of habit we convince ourselves we love what we're doing, but if we truly asked, "What is my perfect calendar? What is the best use of my time, talents and resources?" then we'd come up with a different answer. That's what our personal entrance, growth and exit strategies should be based on—what we really, truly want to do with our lives and who we really want to become.

II

Wealth:
How to Keep It

4

If You Could Have the Perfect Situation: Planning to Achieve Your Goals

Wealth—a blessing for many, a curse for some; but always a challenge for those who care enough to keep it.

Regardless of how you view your wealth, you must be interested in safeguarding and making the most of your wealth if you've picked up this book. During the 15 years that I have been helping wealthy individuals and families make the most of their hard-earned money, one principle that I have learned and would like to share with you is this: Acquiring wealth and maintaining wealth involve different paradigms and mindsets.

It takes different focus, skills and talents to manage and make the most of your money once you've earned it. You can be great at conquering business or competitors and building your business or personal wealth, but then find yourself empty-handed because you neglected to manage your wealth effectively. Estate taxes, capital gains taxes, litigation and other problems can devastate your wealth and peace of mind.

Every once in awhile, far more often than they'd like, celebrities will be in the news because they've declared bankruptcy or run into financial problems. What happened to the great fortunes they amassed? Inattention to details, tax problems, unethical advisors, litigation and personal neglect are among the causes of such misfortunes. However, there is one simple truth we must internalize and accept. *No matter what happens to our money, we must live with the results. After all the blaming is done, our net worth is what it is. No more, no less.* That's the reality we have to live with.

Wealth should be a tool that enables us to reach our lifestyle goals or perfect calendar. Unlike other financial books you'll find on the shelf that try to offer "how-to" help, the purpose of this book is to help empower you through knowledge, examples, experience and a touch of philosophy to make the best decisions possible so that you can keep your wealth and use it to reach your goals. As we journey through this book, we'll discuss goals, strategies, selecting advisors, self-defeating paradigms and important choices. You'll learn how to choose competent advisors and create win/win relationships that fulfill everyone's needs. You may learn to expand your horizons and your ability to identify and achieve true happiness.

I've met a lot of people who have built up large estates and naively thought that when they had x number of dollars, they'd be happy. Then they'd be able to do what they wanted to do. Unfortunately, instead of feeling satisfied and fulfilled, they're worried. They're unhappy. Why? Because they don't have the right vision, strategies and tactics to achieve a better calendar.

Do these objectives seem attractive to you?

- Maximum benefits to you during your lifetime (live the lifestyle you want)

- Maximum benefits to heirs (while you're alive and/or after your death)

- Minimum taxation (avoidance of capital gains taxes, minimization of income taxes, estate taxes and gift taxes)

- The creation of a legacy which provides benefits to your favorite causes or the community instead of simply forfeiting your wealth to Congress (charitable giving through personal benefit tax-exempt trusts, private foundations, etc.)

With proper planning, competent, creative advisors and a personal commitment to action, you will be amazed at just how much better your life can be. You can also provide adequate layers of liability protection for your hard-earned wealth. Peace of mind is very important.

Unfortunately, as I have met with people and discussed the best methods to preserve and use their wealth, I have found some who would rather stay oblivious to the realities of sound wealth management or who refuse to do anything about their situation except complain.

A couple of years ago I met with a potential client in Palm Springs who requested that his wife not be involved in their personal and family strategic planning. I explained that there were two main reasons why that arrangement would not work. First, his wife should have input. Second, it would be very difficult to execute any strategies or documents without her participation. He said, "Well, my wife just doesn't want to do any of this stuff because she says we've already done our estate planning twice. She just wants to have it done with." Based on the information he'd given me, it had been 17 years since they had updated their estate planning. During those 17 years, the laws had changed numerous times, and their children had grown and now had children of their own. So, I asked him, "Haven't your needs and your children's needs changed since then?" He replied, "My wife just doesn't like to do this. She thinks it's just a way for attorneys to make a lot of money." "Then she is going to cost your estate $12 million," I told him, "because that's the amount of your estate tax today based on your current situation. Besides, we're talking about strategic planning and macro wealth management, not just estate planning. We're talking about a big-picture approach to identifying and reaching your goals."

Billions of dollars are lost each year because of a lack of planning or poor, inadequate planning. There is a game being played with your wealth. You can either win the game by being an active participant and creating a plan to win based on various strategies available to you, or you can pretend that no such game exists, take no action and therefore lose by default. The government will take 55% of your estate. You will not receive all of the lifetime benefits you could have had. You cannot win a game you are unwilling to play.

Part of my job is to help clients construct a plan that will enable them to make the most of their money, make it work for them and empower them to reach their goals. We're all supposed to be on the same team fighting a battle we all want to win. We want to employ all the necessary tools and weapons to win that battle.

A person could possess a full arsenal of the tools and weapons necessary to win a battle and still lose the war if he or she refuses to change. The only constant is indeed constant change. Using the battle analogy, when somebody in effect says to me, "We've taken this hill and we're just going to stay here," there's a problem because the battle may now have moved 20 miles away. Everything is always changing. Our needs and priorities change. Our situations change. Tax laws change. Markets change.

If you say, "We intend to win the war, but we're just going to stay right here on this hill. We're not going to change because we're comfortable here," and the war is now 20 miles away, then you need to pack up your stuff and move over to where the war is. You can have a chance to win, or you can sit there on the hill while all the other battles are lost around you and you end up fighting the war all by yourself. You're going to lose. And it will be your own fault.

People often look at taxes and say, "The government is doing all these things to me." The government, in effect, has also provided means and methods of getting around a large portion of taxes; so therefore, the government is only going to be able to confiscate the money of the people who lack knowledge, or those who have the knowledge but lack movement.

You have to be smarter and more *active* than the average millionaire to win this game.

5

Get In, Sit Down

Get in, sit down, hold on and shut up," a stock broker recently told me. She wasn't warning me about her driving, but rather describing the prevailing attitude throughout the financial community. She told me that in essence her job was to sort through all the slickly packaged products and self-centeredness of the financial industry to find the tactics and tools that would really serve her clients' best interests. "It isn't easy," she continued. "They all tell such a promising story. The truth, however, is that some of the stuff in the marketplace won't perform as advertised. Not only is the performance potential exaggerated, but this junk is often bought by the wrong people. Most people, even very wealthy people, haven't got a clue about what to do with their money. Most people have portfolios consisting of stocks, bonds, real estate, etc., and they can't tell you definitively why they bought this stuff, let alone when, why or how they might sell it. There is no rhyme or reason to it, no defined entrance or exit strategy. No structure. No specific goals. It's all so vague and ambiguous. Maybe that's the way the industry wants it. Add that to the fact that people are too lazy or intimidated by complexity, and it's no wonder so few people know where they are and where they want to go with their net worth," she concluded.

As a third-party consultant looking into the investment arena, I had to admit there was a lot of truth in what she had said. In fact, I think that such attitudes toward the consumer run rampant throughout every aspect of our existence. It works something like this, "This is all very complicated, Mr./Ms. investor (legal client, voter, insurance prospect or tax payer). But don't worry, I'll take care of you." The advisors continue on with a dissertation of their own expertise or that of their associates. Sometimes our questions are dismissed or shrugged aside. At other times the answers are patronizing, or even meant to intimidate us or embarrass us into silence. Some professionals (especially politicians) are particularly adept at making up studies, polls or projections that seem to prove their points of view. There is an old saying, "They say that figures don't lie, but have you ever noticed how liars sure can figure?" In essence, they want us to get in, sit down, hold on and shut up.

"Many professionals," she lamented about her colleagues, "just want clients to 'get in, sit down, hold on and shut up'."

There are people in decision-making positions who determine the atmosphere and the attitude by which ideas will be conveyed to the public. In the financial services industry, these are at least in part the people who decide what investment products are going to be marketed to the public. They publish articles and place advertising. We can look historically at the legal, investment, insurance and accounting professions and see clear trends in "hot" marketing items. For a while, the accounting industry was promoting tax projections—getting your taxes done in the middle of the current year rather than waiting until after January of the next year to determine what your taxes might be. In the legal profession, living trusts were aggressively marketed in the 1970s through the mid-1980s. In the Los Angeles area during that time, you could not pick up a major newspaper without seeing at least one and in some cases three or four advertisements each day for living trust seminars. Although there are still living trust seminars going on, the heyday of the living trust phenomenon has run its course. What's the latest, hottest ticket in the legal profession today? Recently it's been the asset protection trust and the family limited partnership. In the investment community, derivatives are an example of a new way of repackaging and redefining certain investment elements so they could arguably deliver growth, income or some combination thereof.

Industries try to come up with products they think will be profitable, marketable and beneficial—or at least capable of being perceived as beneficial—to the public. Most products are not inherently bad. For example, I think tax projections are a good idea. Some of the insurance products and annuity products the insurance industry is out there hyping on a consistent basis are really good. We've got life insurance, disability insurance, business insurance and the whole gamut of homeowner's and umbrella policies. Some of these forms of coverage are essential to protecting and preserving one's wealth, business and/or shareholders. But do you know what is beneficial for you and what is not? Are your advisors looking out for your best interest or trying to sell you a product?

When Orange County, Calif., declared bankruptcy as a result of participating in a poorly administered investment policy, I had to ask the question, "If the investment executives, advisors and elected officials were truly capable and competent, would they have sat by and let Orange County, or the controller and treasurer of Orange County, overexpose the county to such undue levels of risk?" On a regular basis, people or organizations invest in areas that are too risky or too conservative for their own good, yet the investment industry is right there to keep selling those investments with little, if any, concern for their suitability.

Although I've been using financial services professionals, accountants and attorneys as examples, this is not to impugn any of those industries or professions on a broad basis. It simply points out that there are *some* people who really do not care about the individual. They care about profits for their company and their own financial status. They want us to "get in, sit down, hold on and shut up." This attitude is not unique to the type of advisors discussed above, but is prevalent in our society.

I recently experienced the "get in, sit down, hold on and shut up" attitude with my ex-dentist. He seemed to be a knowledgeable person and had graduated from one of the finest dental schools in the country. I had no reason to doubt his abilities, and his office was convenient, so I became his patient. I saw him on a number of occasions and everything was fine. Then one day, he told me I would need a series of treatments including root planing and a number of other things that didn't sound terribly pleasant. In typical dentist fashion, he assured me that the treatments wouldn't be really painful; I would feel some "discomfort." Besides sounding more than uncomfortable to me, the treatments were also expensive. I told the dentist I would think about it. Then I stuck to one of my top ten rules: Get a second opinion on anything painful, expensive, or important.

One of my longtime friends had bought out his father's dental practice. I went to see him for a second opinion. He examined me, took x-rays and told me he couldn't see any problem. He couldn't imagine that I would need the drastic treatments the other dentist was recommending. He called in two other dentists from his office to take a look at my x-rays and examine my teeth, and they rendered the same opinion. Not having had an opportunity beforehand to "get their stories straight," I was impressed by their consistency and did not doubt the truthfulness of their opinions. Obviously, I did not need to undergo the treatments suggested by the first dentist.

As a consumer, how do you know when somebody is telling you the truth? There are professionals who prey upon other people. They're going to try to take advantage of our ignorance, and they're going to try to intimidate or manipulate us into cooperating with them and doing what they want us to do. Many times they're recommending an option not because it's beneficial for us, but simply because it's profitable for them, either in money terms or in garnering more power and influence. (To people with a lot of money, the power and influence are often more important.)

Arrogance and manipulation occur all around us. If we act as though they don't exist or if we try to shelter ourselves, we're going to get hurt. We're going to end up getting dental treatments that we don't need, investments that are not in our best interest or legal documents that do not carry out our intended purpose. We can end up with politicians and bureaucrats who betray our trust and the Constitution. In some cases, we're going to end up with very serious disasters as a result of our own unwillingness to consider the facts and face the truth.

I don't mean to imply that all professionals act this way. But as a consumer like me, you've probably had enough of such arrogant and condescending attitudes. Over the past decade or so, I've had the pleasure to meet and work with professionals who are also tired of the status quo, tired of the system as it is now. We want to change the way business gets done in this country by educating the public. But that is only one step in the right direction. The most important step is the assumption of responsibility by consumers. It is time for an economic revolution. At the very least, it is time for *your* economic evolution.

So, how can you tell if you're getting what you really need? First, you have to realize that not everyone is recommending options based on your best interest. If I've been able to convince you that this happens, the next thing I want to convey is that it's probably happening to you right now. You probably have people around you today who are rendering advice, managing your assets or looking out for your dental well-being who are looking out for themselves first and you second. Perhaps it's not that severe and your advisors aren't putting themselves first, but they still may not be fully pushing for your best interest either. Perhaps they're just going through the motions. Even if that's the case, you still get hurt. If you're not sure the people you're dealing with are looking out for you, you need to ask yourself some hard questions: "Who is the center of the universe for this advisor? When this person is representing me, am I the center of his or her universe? Is my situation uppermost in his or her mind? Or am I just a meal-ticket for this attorney, accountant, financial planner, doctor, whoever this person might be? Do they really care about me as an individual?" The large majority of advisors really haven't got a clue about you as a person, what you want to do, what your life is all about or anything truly meaningful about you. So how can these people adequately represent you?

This brings us to the next part of the test, one that very few professionals can pass. The next time you have the opportunity (you might even create the opportunity) to talk to your attorney, accountant, stock broker, financial planner, insurance agent or any other advisor, *ask if you can see their file copy of your goals and objectives.* You as an individual are trying to accomplish something. You're trying to get somewhere other than where you are right now. Are your advisors able to articulate your position? Can they say where you are today, why you're there, whether or not you're happy being there, and if you're not happy where you are, what direction you want to go in? What are your goals and objectives? If they can't provide an articulated response to your inquiry, then you have to ask yourself, "If these people don't know these things about me, these very important core issues about me, how can they possibly represent my best interest?"

As I teach continuing education courses to attorneys, accountants, stock brokers, financial planners and the like, I try very hard to convey this important message to them: It is essential for them to help their clients find and articulate their goals and objectives so that a written record of these goals and objectives can be kept in their files. I present the idea to professionals in this way: "Think of your top 25 clients, the very best, most important clients. Can you pull their files and tell me within five minutes what the clients' goals and objectives are, what's important to them in their lives and what their personal mission statements are?" Across the board, professionals everywhere with very few exceptions look at me as if I'm from another planet. They tell me they've never heard of such a thing. They do not have any such record. In fact, they will say to me, "How do you expect me to have something like that when none of my clients know what the heck they're doing or what they want?"

Picture a courtroom, if you will, where a lawsuit has been filed against a professional. You, the plaintiff, are claiming malfeasance of some nature. You're telling the judge, "My advisor didn't look out for my best interest. She messed this up and it cost me x amount of money. She should have known that these investments were not suitable for me. She should have known that this particular tactic or tool was going to expose me to an undue level of risk which I could not tolerate." The attorney for the defense approaches you and says, "Perhaps you can tell the court what your goals and objectives are. Perhaps *you* can articulate that for us." If you can't articulate your own goals and objectives, you're going to have a pretty difficult time winning your case. If you don't know what it is you're doing, where you are, where you want to go and how you want to get there, it's pretty ridiculous to think that you could hire a professional, pay her x amount of money and expect her to read your mind and guess right on all these important issues.

I met with a father and a son who were trying to buy out the family agriculture business from the dad's two sisters. Their accountant had done a beautiful overview of how they should go about this transaction. Our firm was hired to give a second opinion and review all the information, to make sure all the T's were crossed and the I's were dotted. I looked at the strategic plan put forward by the accountant and I thought, "This is fabulous. This is one of the most articulate, in-depth plans I've ever seen. I would actually outsource some work to that accounting firm." It was done that well. I told everybody that when we all got together. The clients, the accountant and the financial advisor were all happy to hear what a great plan they had in front of them.

When we all sat down in the financial advisor's office, I said, "This is a great overview. The T's are crossed, the I's are dotted and everything is ready to go. I just have a few questions for you."

I looked over at the dad and asked, "If you could just get a check in the mail every month, how much total annual income net after taxes do you think you would be able to live on comfortably?"

He said, "Well, I would need about $75,000 a year."

I asked the son the same question and he said $125,000 a year. I asked the father what his net worth was and he said it was about $6 million, most of it tied up in the family agricultural business. The son's net worth was about $4 million, most of it again tied up in the family agricultural business. Next I asked, "If you could create the perfect calendar and you could live the lifestyle you really want; if you could spend your time, talent and resources doing exactly what you want to do, whenever you want to do it; if you could get rid of all the activities that you don't want to do, what would that perfect calendar look like?"

They both sat back in their chairs, and the dad said, "Well, I never really thought about that before."

"Well, give it some thought," I told them. "What really important things would you like to do with your time, talent and resources?"

So we started listing their key activities. Finally I asked them both, "Is there anything missing? Anything that isn't on this list?"

They said, "No, we don't think so. We've got all the big things, anyway."

I said, "O.K., it's kind of hard to answer that question all at one time. But how about spending 70 hours a week running an agricultural business? I don't see that on the list for your perfect calendar." The dad said, "Well, you said if it was the perfect calendar and we could do whatever we wanted to do."

I said, "Yes, that's the question I asked."

And then the son got it. It was like watching a cartoon where the light bulb goes off above somebody's head. He looked at his dad and said, "Dad, we've got to get on the same page. We're not living the lives we really want to live. We've got everything tied up in the business and what we're about to do is take our $10 million of net worth, pledge it as collateral and borrow another $20 million so we can buy out Aunt Sylvia and Aunt Mary. The point is, we could be living our perfect calendar if we got out of that business too."

The father said, "I never thought of that. I thought I was just going to work at the business until I die."

At this point the accountant joined the conversation. He said to the son, "You mentioned that we need to be on the same page. We are on the same page. In fact, you have 50 pages of analysis, recommendations and summary of the same page." The accountant was noticeably irritated with the clients, with the direction of the conversation and with me.

As lovingly as possible, I reaffirmed the fine job he and his firm had done. Then I pointed out that there was only one problem with the analysis: The accountant had let the client incorrectly define the mission. This is an all too common problem with the communication between clients and advisors. Clients don't always know what the real questions or right issues are. But the client defines the issues as well as the advisor's role . . . and together they march right down the wrong path.

What I am offering as a new paradigm is this: *Let's get on the right page.* You must make sure that you and the people you work with are on the "right page" and moving in the best direction for you. The left-brain financial analysis offered by the accountant had not taken into account the critical right-brain issues necessary to move the clients to a higher level of fulfillment and quality of life.

This is just one of many examples of people lacking "the right page," a macro strategic plan or entrance, growth and exit strategies. For these millionaires, life was mostly about going to work every day. By redefining the game, we help people see that the real game is about the quality of life, not just about success in business or making more money than they can or will ever spend.

In fact, money really shouldn't be anything but the means to become free enough to pursue the life you've always wanted. But most people haven't got a clue how to define that perfect (or even just better) calendar and life. They need expert coaching and guidance to get them from where they are to the position where they have a vision—some would say a clue—as to who they are and what they want to be when they grow beyond their job.

After completing his macro strategic planning and coaching process, a 75-year-old client made this observation, "Hey, I guess what this comes down to is, what am I going to be when I grow up?" Please understand, it's not about how old we are, it's about how evolved we are!

There's a mutual responsibility here. You, as the client, need to know what your goals and objectives are and to tell your advisors. Your advisors need to ask you what your goals and objectives are and work toward them. A tremendous communication gap exists. The professionals know it would be helpful to them and their clients to know their clients' goals and objectives, but sometimes it's uncomfortable for the professional to bring the subject up and pursue it, especially if the client becomes hostile when the professional broaches the subject. A lot of clients will respond, "That's too personal. I don't want to talk about that. I don't want to talk about goals and objectives; I just want to talk about what's the most effective way to sell my business without having to pay taxes on it." Of course, the really dedicated, highly competent professional will not allow the dialogue to move forward without dealing with the big picture issues. But it's really an elite group of professionals, a very small, limited percentage of the professionals in any discipline, who have the fortitude to look a client in the eye and say, "Look, I can't represent your best interest if I don't know what your best interest is. If all I'm doing is looking at a single transaction in a vacuum, I can't possibly give you good advice. We have to look at the big picture and examine your goals in order to determine whether this individual transaction is good or bad for you." If you as a client try to avoid these issues, you're going to hurt yourself.

The stock broker at the beginning of this chapter who described her industry's philosophy as "get in, sit down, hold on and shut up" is an example of a professional who, when she stepped back from it all and took a look at her industry, realized that the majority of the behavior within that industry is self-centered. The majority of that behavior is designed for profitability in the short term for the industry rather than long-term relationship building and long-term profitability for the consumer/client. She has established herself as a true professional representing the best interests of her clients. She makes them the center of the universe, and therefore she is rewarded accordingly. That is perhaps the highest level that a professional can obtain. In so doing she has achieved a sustainable competitive advantage over would-be competitors.

In my discussions with her, she told me that she turns down a lot of business because there are many consumers who tend to use people and take unfair advantage of professionals. She will not do business with people who are not relationship-oriented and who do not have a high degree of integrity. So it's really a two-way street. If you want to play ball at the very highest level of performance, if you want to be represented by the best people possible, you have to be worthy of that representation. I believe that clients and professionals who are looking for long-term, successful relationships must possess and display personal integrity and a commitment to an "everyone must win" philosophy. But before a relationship can become truly successful, both the advisor and the client need to know the client's goals.

6

Seeing the Big Picture

There is an old tale from India which tells of a wise Rajah who made a study of human nature. The Rajah gathered six blind men together and asked them to describe the animal in front of them. Since all six men had been blind since birth, they had never seen an elephant.

The first man touched the tusk and said, "This animal is like a spear." The second man felt the trunk and declared, "This animal is like a snake." Feeling the ear, the third man exclaimed, "This animal is like a fan." The fourth man stroked the elephant's front leg and announced, "This animal is like a tree." The fifth man, after patting the elephant's side, decided, "This animal is like a wall." Finally, the sixth man grasped the tail and proclaimed, "This animal is like a rope."

The six blind men began arguing over who was right and who was wrong. Because each of these men had an ego and pride, as most of us do, the argument became quite heated. At this point, the Rajah stepped in and said, "The elephant is a large animal, made up of different parts. Each of you has knowledge of only one part. To find out the whole truth, you must gain knowledge of all the parts and put them all together. In order to do this, you must set aside your ego and pride to realize you may not have all the knowledge necessary to comprehend the whole elephant."

This story exemplifies the essence of macro or big-picture thinking.

In some ways, we can all be like the blind men. Trying to get an accurate perspective or find the truth in life, finance, etc., can be very difficult, especially if we are too

close to the problem. Often true perspective and full knowledge are gained only when we step back from a situation
and try to look at it from all angles. In order to do this
effectively, we often need help for several reasons. First, if
it's about *us*

We need to learn to see the whole elephant.

or *our* situation, the closer we are to an issue, the more
emotional we tend to be. The more emotional we become,
the less objective we are. Second, we cannot be experts in
everything. We don't know what all the angles are or everything to look for. Thus, we often need third-party help
to accurately perceive and overcome obstacles.

When I am introduced to a new client, the conversation
usually begins with a very particular problem to solve. People
tend to focus on one specific issue, not the whole picture.
They want to know how to fix that prominent problem now,
yet rarely is it in the client's best interest to proceed immediately with solutions. Many people don't realize that every
action they take concerning their assets is likely to affect
their entire net worth. Therefore, it is crucial that we have
a clear understanding of the "whole elephant," the complete
personal long-term goals, before we undertake any critical
changes. It is even safer to say, before we undertake *any*
changes. Most people do not know enough about financial
issues, tax law, etc., to discern what is critical and what is
not, and what all of the ramifications might be.

For example, I often meet people who, after obtaining
more knowledge and perspective, wish they had not financed
a certain property or other asset. They discover too late

that financing can greatly reduce options and flexibility or increase tax liability upon certain transfers or liquidation. Suppose a person who lacks knowledge and/or perspective decides to finance an asset and pursues a loan through a bank or other lender. It is very unlikely that the lender will question the applicant to see if financing is really the best thing for the person to do. It is also unlikely that the lender will fully and properly inform the applicant of all options available, rather than just those which directly apply to financing. The lender is not concerned with the applicant's big-picture goals and long-term future interests over multiple generations. In fact, I've never met anyone in the lending business who was adequately trained to identify and explore the macro picture. They are neither trained nor compensated to look at the whole elephant. The lender just wants to make good, repayable loans. The applicant thinks he or she wants a loan. That's a good enough match for everyone, at least for now. It's only later that the client may discover that such financing may have been the worst thing she could have done based upon her big picture needs.

So, how do we gain perspective? How do we begin to see the big picture and focus on long-term goals? It's hard to think too far down the road, because most people pursue short-term objectives. They live in the here and now.

Long-term success requires a certain boldness and maturity. We must understand the risks of new choices *and* the risks of inaction. There is risk in action and inaction alike. The Chinese have only one symbol to represent both risk and opportunity. Perhaps one of our greatest challenges in life in general, as well as in finance, is to recognize one from the other. Sometimes it takes great courage to change a direction or take action. Sometimes the greatest danger or the position of guaranteed loss is staying where we are currently comfortable. For example, an investment that seems safe in terms of protection of principal may not be so safe after one considers the effects of inflation combined with taxes, or what some professionals refer to as "tax-flation."

Perhaps the best way to explain tax-flation is to show an example. Let's say you deposit $100,000 into a time deposit or other interest-bearing account with a bank, credit union or savings and loan, or purchase a government security such as a T-Bill, GNMA, etc. Next, we'll assume an effective annual yield of 6%. We must also select a tax bracket and an inflation rate. Let's use a tax bracket of 35% (combined federal and state) and an inflation rate of 4%. This information applied to the following formula will give us our Internal Rate of Return (net after tax, after inflation rate of return).

Internal Rate of Return

$100,000
x   6%   (Interest Rate)
= 6,000   (Interest Yield)
-   Taxes   (at 35% = $2,100)
= 3,900   (Net after tax)
-Inflation   ($100,000 x 4% = $4,000)
=   -100   (Internal rate of return net/net)

Net after tax yield   3,900 (3.9%)
Less inflation loss   4,000 (Loss of purchasing power)
                      =-100 (Negative internal rate of return)

As you can see, such a position is mathematically un-sound, a guaranteed loss. Far too often people put money into such accounts seeking security when in fact they're losing purchasing power. You must be aware of the Internal Rate of Return (IRR) on your entire net worth. It is easy to see how under such economic conditions the perception of safety is entirely an illusion. A guaranteed loss hardly equates to safety. It's hard to find anything "riskier" than a guaranteed loss.

Breaking out of a short-sighted mold, limited perspective, or short-term approach is difficult but essential to success. The best way to do this is to establish a 100-year plan.

7

Your 100-Year Plan

When we're taking a look at overall planning, strategies and so forth, we have to realize that we have different needs at different times. Psychological theorist Abraham Maslow believed we have a tremendous potential for personal development. However, there are certain needs that have to be satisfied before we can reach what he called "self-actualization," the point at which we become the best that we can be. Maslow developed a "hierarchy of needs" triangle that demonstrates the different levels of human needs:

The first level is survival. You've got to put food in your mouth, a roof over your head, and clothes on your body. When you're at this level, you think, "I'll dig ditches 12 hours a day if I just could have some food in my belly and a warm, dry place to sleep at night." So you start to dig ditches, but then after awhile, your belly is full and you begin to become disgruntled. You see the guy who's in charge of all of the people digging ditches and you think, "Gee, he's got a better life than I do. I wish I could do that." And you begin to elevate your concerns and get away from fundamental survival and into other more rewarding, evolved levels.

Maslow's hierarchy of needs is relevant to understanding people's level of acceptance or readiness to participate in macro strategic planning or in advanced wealth management. The first priority should be to provide for myself and my wife during our lifetimes, making the most of what we have so that we never want for anything. I don't know what our health is going to be, physically or mentally, five years from now or 50 years from now, and I have an obligation to my children and society to ensure that my wife and I will not become a burden to other people. A lot of people have become burdens to society or burdens to future generations because they have failed to secure their own positions.

The next priority is an emotional, philosophical and partly a timing decision and that is, "What am I going to do with the assets over and above what my wife and I need?" Personally, I still have children at home, and I believe it's my responsibility to make sure that my children do not become a burden to anyone else or to society. So I have implemented and funded tactics and strategies which take care of my children to the extent that I want them provided for.

With any excess assets over and above that, I believe, I have a moral obligation to direct any excess money to viable causes rather than to the State government or Congress. If you are financially successful, there's a portion of your wealth that you cannot freely give to your children even if you want to. Uncle Sam won't let you. Your only choices for that particular amount are to give it to charity or to Congress in the form of taxes.

If you believe that the government is the best steward for your money, or at least 55% of your money, then don't do anything. Do what you're doing now, and the government will take the money and spend it on all kinds of things you disagree with. Because of your lack of action or your lack of knowledge, you will choose Congress over your preferred causes by default. But you have a choice.

Capital gains and estate taxes are in fact options, not mandates. You can choose to designate what cause(s) your wealth will support if you plan for it now and make it a part of your agenda. You can use the portion of your wealth that would have gone to Uncle Sam and put it back into your community, finance a legacy or a personal or family mission.

Creating Your Plan

The primary definition of estate planning in this country is, "When you're dead, how are you going to divide up your stuff?" But that's only Level 1 of estate planning. Level 2 is, "You have an estate while you're alive, so what can you do to make the most of your money while you're alive to benefit you and your family now and during the course of your lifetime? And then after you pass away, what are you going to do to distribute this money effectively, and to whom and where will it be distributed?" That's a better approach than Level 1, but there's a higher level, a Level 3, where I think the game really ought to be played. Level 3 is far more valuable than "estate planning" and has far more substance to it, and that is, "What's your 100-year plan? What are you going to be doing while you're alive to fulfill your 100-year plan and how is that going to be carried on after your passing?"

Basically, the 100-year plan breaks down into two parts:

- The balance of your lifetime

- After you're dead

For example, if your estimated life expectancy were another 25 years, your plan would break down as follows:

- 25-year lifetime legacy (what you want to do while you're alive)

- 75-year family and community legacy (what you want your wealth to accomplish after you've passed away)

It's not just an issue of taking care of yourself or distributing money to your heirs; it goes way beyond that to creating a legacy while you're alive and furthering that legacy after you pass on. If you're 60 years old when I meet you, you may think a 100-year plan doesn't make sense for you, but it really does. If you can get your heirs to accept this 100-year philosophy of life, then how much more effective are you going to be and how much more effective are they going to be? The big-picture questions raise us out of the mundane, rudimentary existence which most people lead, the day-to-day, moment-to-moment existence. How do you define success? How do you really achieve fulfillment? You find happiness and fulfillment by being of value and offering service to other people or to viable, worthwhile causes, purposes and missions.

When people begin to think in terms of their 100-year plan, there is often a profound impact on their lives and the lives of countless others because their plans become bigger than just themselves or bigger than just them and their families.

Think of these words, recorded in *Four Minute Essays, Volume IV*, by Dr. Frank Crane:

Make no little plans.
They have no magic to
stir men's blood and
probably themselves
will not be realized.
Make big plans. Aim
high in hope and work,
remembering that a
noble, logical diagram
once recorded will
never die, but
long after we are gone
will be a living thing
asserting itself, with
ever growing insistency.
Remember that our sons
and grandsons are going
to do things that would
stagger us. Let your
watchword be order and
your beacon, beauty.

D. Burnham

The Lifetime Legacy

The first part of the 100-year plan, the "lifetime legacy," should focus on your perfect calendar as well as your personal and family goals and aspirations during your lifetime. Your finances should be arranged (perhaps changed) to allow you full implementation/realization of these goals. In order to take full advantage of this type of plan, we must dare to dream. We will absolutely require third-party assistance for this because we don't know all that's possible for us. We must create a macro strategic plan in order to replace the chaos.

It would be wonderful if we had a financial advisor who was also a psychologist, because this part of the planning process requires us to use the right side of our brains. As you probably know, research has shown that the two hemispheres of our brain are different. The right hemisphere is more creative and emotional, while the left hemisphere is more analytical and logical. The trick is to get the two sides of our brain to work together when setting and achieving goals. We need to use the right side of our brains to dream up and think of all the possibilities available to us, and then use the left side of our brains to help us rationally form a plan to reach or accomplish those goals. Think about your own situation. Are you left-brain or right-brain dominant? Are you more creative or analytical? If you tend to be more creative and emotional, then you're probably right-brain dominant. If you think you're in the middle or can't decide, don't worry. Maybe you're pretty well balanced. You will benefit greatly if you and your advisors use a whole-brain rather than a half-brained approach.

The Family/Community Legacy

The second part of the 100-year plan, the "family/community legacy," deals with what happens after you've died. What can you do with your wealth to benefit your family and the community? This part of the plan deals with issues, people and causes that are nearest and dearest to you (right-brain issues) and the most effective means to address and benefit those people and causes (left-brain issues).

A properly executed 100-year plan is a balance of left- and right-brain issues. Balanced thinking is critical to success. If all of this seems complicated and difficult, you're not alone. Anything great or worthwhile is difficult. If this were not true, everyone would be great and happy. True happiness requires effort, thought and boldness of heart. Happiness also requires a well thought out list of goals and an accompanying strategic plan to carry them out.

At times, this long-term, macro strategic planning seems overwhelming, complicated and difficult. Perhaps we can take some consolation in this thought: You can't expect to deal with all the macro issues and tie up all the loose ends overnight. Instead of becoming overwhelmed by complication, fear, analysis paralysis, etc., establish a timeline for your macro and micro planning and execution. Your timeline should set realistic goals for:

1. Gathering and assimilating information on goal setting.

2. Establishing written, specific, articulate goals.

3. Developing your perfect calendar.

4. Drafting macro and micro strategic plans to carry out those goals.

5. Implementing the planning.

6. Systematically reviewing the goals and execution timeline.

7. Systematically adjusting the vision, goals, strategies, tactics, tools and timing.

With a proper attitude, more knowledge, objective help and an adequate balance of left- and right-brain thought, we can all become more effective, successful and happy. What's more, with a 100-year plan, we can be instrumental in the success of many others. It is a necessary part of the fulfillment of human existence to be engaged in something bigger than ourselves. A 100-year plan makes all of this possible, but only if we have the strength of mind, character and competency to put it into action.

8

Where Are You Headed?

Let's get right to the point. What is your money *really*
doing for you? Did you ever say to yourself, "Someday when
I have more money, I'll ..."? Have you actually done the things
you always hoped to do? Are you doing what you want to do
now? Do you spend your time, talents and resources doing
what you want to do? What are your goals? If you could
have the perfect situation, what would it be?

These are the questions I ask all of my clients in order to
achieve proper vision. Getting a concise, articulate list of
goals usually requires a lot more probing on my part, however. Most often the answers to these questions are tangled
in the individual's perception of how things currently are.
When setting goals, people are often influenced by other
people's opinions, or limited by what they think they already
know about money, tax law, etc. For example, many people
tell me they would love to sell a problematic building or stock.
But then they say, "The capital gains tax is so high that I
just can't sell it." They don't know there are several tactics
they could implement to eliminate the capital gains tax on
the sale of such assets. A person's lack of knowledge or mis-
conception of technical issues limits that person's options.

We are all trapped by our limited knowledge. It is this
limitation which ultimately interferes with our ability to
achieve wide-angle macro vision, to dream, set goals or move
ahead. When clients say they cannot sell an appreciated asset without paying capital gains taxes, I could immediately
jump into a "teacher" mode and explain various techniques
for avoiding the payment of capital gains taxes. However, it

is more helpful to stay focused on defining the goals and then explain the various techniques or tactics after all of the goals are identified. It took me a while to figure this out. Proper vision and goal definition are so important that they must come first. If we cannot articulate *and* stand by our vision and goals, we become moving targets. No one can help us, and we cannot help ourselves if we keep changing our mind or redefining our goals. It is crucial that we devote the necessary time to establish goals which are true to our wide-angle vision and to what we ultimately desire so that we can stick to them. When developing your goals, remember that you can still build in enough flexibility to allow for changes and your own evolution.

So just how can we work together to overcome the many obstacles which would interfere with our vision and goal-setting process? It's really rather simple and can be summed up with this question: "If you could wave a magic wand, and completely ignore the tax and investment laws (or your perception of them), what would your perfect situation be?" We need to free ourselves of our misconceptions and ignore what we think we know, and concentrate on what we really want.

We also need to make sure that we are actually setting goals and not just focusing on strategies. Think of a football game. When a football team enters the field, its goal is to win the game. However, there may be several strategies it employs to achieve that goal depending on the strengths and weaknesses of the team, its opponent and the circumstances. The goal or objective is the desired end result: to win. The strategy and tactics are the means used to achieve the goal. The same is true in the advanced wealth management game. The strategies available to help you keep your wealth will be fulfilled through a variety of tactics—trusts, partnerships, foundations, etc. However, when setting financial lifestyle goals, many people forget to concentrate on the goals and spend too much time concentrating on the strategies, or worse, the tools.

I recently met a man named Charlie who was literally replacing his goal with a tactic. When I first talked to him, he said his goal was to structure the sale of his business in such a way that he could sell it to his son-in-law and maintain a consulting relationship so that he could contribute at least $100,000 a year to his qualified plan. I asked him why he wanted to continue contributions to his qualified plan. He replied, "I want enough retirement income."

I was able to help him understand that what he wanted, his goal, was to have enough net after tax income to be free of financial worries. That was his objective. I explained that making contributions to a qualified plan was a tactic, not a goal. He thought he wanted to put $100,000 a year into his qualified plan. He thought that was his goal. However, he was employing that tactic to reach an actual goal—to acquire retirement income. Unfortunately for him, what he was doing was totally out of harmony with his goals because he already had more money in his qualified plan than he should have had. He was overfunded. He actually needed to strip money out of his qualified plan. He had limited himself by his lack of knowledge; he had no macro plan and no appropriate exit strategy.

Another one of his goals was to pass as much money as he could to his children. However, if he continued to accumulate money in his qualified plan, the tax at the time of distribution to his kids could have been close to 85%. Obviously, that tactic or form of title was not the most beneficial for his children.

Charlie was focusing on the tactic as if it were a goal. After further evaluation and education, Charlie realized that putting more money into his qualified plan would actually hurt his real goals—acquiring maximum retirement income and passing as much of his wealth as possible to his children and favored causes.

When we set goals, we need to make sure they're really goals and not tactics. One way to make sure you're focusing on a goal and not a tactic is to ask yourself, "Why am I doing this?" If it's a tactic, your answer will often lead you to the goal you're actually trying to achieve. For example, when I asked Charlie why he was putting $100,000 in his qualified plan, he realized that his answer—"I want enough retirement income"—was really the goal. In part, Charlie's thinking was clouded because years earlier someone had completely sold him on qualified plans. Charlie needed help to see that he had outgrown that tactic.

Besides asking the question, "Why am I doing this?," another clue to identifying goals is to recognize that goals tend to have emotional, psychological or philosophical undertones. Charlie said he wanted enough retirement income. Underlying this goal was an emotional need to be free of financial worries. He didn't want to worry about his own well-being or his wife's. He also wanted to benefit his children because of his emotional ties to them. He wanted to help them be free of financial worries and to take care of them.

Some people may argue that you cannot establish firm goals because things are always changing. People who would make such an argument are confusing goals with strategy. For example, one of my goals may be to always have enough income to maintain a certain lifestyle. In order to accomplish this goal, I will need to employ various strategies. These strategies must evolve as things change. However, it is very unlikely that my goal to maintain the lifestyle that I want will change. Thus, my goal remains constant, but my strategies, tactics and tools *must* change over time.

We all ultimately want to be free, not just from financial worries, but to be free to pursue what we really want to do with our lives. Maybe we want to travel or give gifts to our grandchildren. Maybe there's a cause we want to support. Maybe we want the freedom to say, "I want to have a 50th anniversary party at the Hyatt hotel in Maui, and I want to pay the airfare and hotel expenses for all of our family and friends." Those are goals and objectives. Using strategies to make the most of our wealth should enable us to achieve our goals.

One of our clients has a goal to rent the Concorde jet for New Year's Eve of the year 2000. He wants to start in New York and experience the arrival of the year 2000 in New York, then California, and then in Hawaii. Our job is to help him use various strategies, tactics and tools to maximize his wealth so that he's able to see this goal become a reality. It is up to his advisors to help him manage his wealth and ensure that he's in a financial position to do this. It's your advisor's job to help you use your wealth to accomplish your goals. However, both you and your advisors need to know what your goals are before they can help you make them reality.

9

Your Perfect Situation

Now it's time for you to define your perfect situation. Most people require some coaching because there is still a tendency to get bogged down in our old thought processes or paradigms and incomplete and/or inaccurate perceptions of tax or investment laws or regulations. I often find myself playing the role of coach, and it is always a challenge. It is much easier on everyone if the client sticks to the open-minded "magic wand, perfect situation" approach discussed in the last chapter.

Remember, when considering a strategic plan to better control your wealth, the best way to begin is to put aside any preconceived ideas about tax laws and to focus instead on vision and goals. Ask yourself, "If I could have the perfect situation, what would it be?" It's the advisor's job to provide the client with the appropriate strategies, tactics, tools and timeline to bring the ideas to fruition.

Good advisors will offer suggestions which might help clients expand their vision of what the perfect situation might be. Often, clients don't know all that is possible and/or don't realize the assumptions they're making about their lives. Many advisors watch in frustration as clients flounder around, trapped in their assumptions because they won't take advantage of the advisor's knowledge and experience.

Describing one's perfect situation is usually not an easy task. Years ago, I did a lot of consulting work for executives of a large aerospace firm in Southern California. The easiest way for me to help them stretch their minds to allow for a productive discussion about their perfect situation was to ask them this question: "Where do you want to live once you retire?"

Usually they would respond, "Where I live now." So the exercise continued with my next question: "If you could pick anywhere in the world to live, why would you choose Burbank?" Often their reply would be, "Because it's close to work." Most of the time I would have to point out what should have been obvious: Once they retired in a couple of months, being close to work would become irrelevant.

That's when the conversation always began to get really interesting. One client named Susan responded, "I've never thought about it like that before. I've always wanted to live right by the ocean." My next question was, "Which ocean?"

Looking at me as if I was really dense, she said, "The Pacific Ocean, Bruce, where else?" So I asked her, "Which coast of the Pacific Ocean?"

Then she said, "Now, Bruce, don't be silly, obviously I mean the west coast, where else?"

The paradigm shift really began with my next question, "Well, if you lived in Hawaii, you could live on the Pacific coast, north, south, east or west, couldn't you?"

Then the light bulb went on—the great "Ah-hah!" The paradigm shift.

"You mean I could live in Hawaii?" she asked. "That would be incredible." Almost immediately, of course, the left brain began to sabotage the right. All her fears and doubts came into play. "How will I see my children and grandchildren?"

I explained. "By converting your less productive assets such as your $10 million of low income-producing stock and undeveloped land into a productive income stream, you can afford to live anywhere in the world you want to. You can have three or four homes around the world. Then you can afford to send your family airline tickets whenever you like. In fact, you can control when they come and when they leave!"

Without such coaching, there would have been no paradigm shift and Susan would never seriously have considered living in Hawaii. She would have been stuck in her little house in Burbank. Her money would not be effectively used for her benefit. She and her family would be living less enjoyable and fulfilling lives.

There's a checklist I use to help clients start thinking about what their perfect situation would be. But before we start the checklist, remember that most estate plans focus on "death benefits" for others rather than on "lifetime benefits" for you now, while you're *alive*. Truly advanced wealth management focuses first on your vision and lifetime benefits—your goals and dreams—and then addresses the distribution of your wealth to others upon your death. This checklist is divided into two categories: your "Life Estate," which concerns your goals and dreams for you now while you're alive, and your "Death Estate," which concerns the distribution of your estate according to your wishes after you pass away.

The first set of questions deals with how you feel. Only you can answer these emotional, philosophical and spiritual questions. They will help you establish your basic goals and should be answered before you take a look at the next set of questions.

Emotional, Philosophical and Spiritual

Questions for Your Lifetime Legacy

- Do I spend my time, talents and resources doing what I really want to do?

- Am I spending my time and talents on the most important things possible?

- If I could spend my time doing anything in the world, what would it be?

- Do I live exactly where I want to live?

- Do I travel whenever and wherever I want?

- Is there a cause I would like to be involved in?

- Do I give intelligently to those in need?

- Do I have any dreams I have not yet accomplished?

- If I could change any list of things in this world, what would they be?

- Do I want to give cash or assets to my heirs while I'm alive?

- If I give to my heirs now, how can I do so without hurting them?

Questions for Your Family and Community Legacy

- How much do I want to distribute and to whom?
- If married, do I want assets distributed to heirs at my death or wait until after my spouse dies?
- If married, what does my spouse want to happen should I die first?
- Are there any causes I would like to provide funding for?
- Rather than pay taxes, would I like to direct my would-be tax dollars to my favored causes?

Be sure you've answered the above questions before you move on to the next set of questions. I call the following questions "pragmatic." They deal with the nuts and bolts of what you want to do. Your advisors can help you answer many of the pragmatic questions. But please remember to concentrate on and answer the emotional, philosophical and spiritual questions first. Those answers provide the foundation to your goals. The pragmatic questions are issues that need to be addressed to make sure your emotional, philosophical and spiritual goals can be met.

Pragmatic

Questions for Your Life Estate

- Do I have more after-tax income than I can possibly spend each month?
- Am I still working when I don't need to be?
- Am I spending my time and talents on the most important things possible?
- Is my net worth balanced to protect me from inflation, deflation, and economic depression?
- If I become physically or mentally disabled, will I be more than adequately provided for?
- Will my current legal structures protect me, my family, if applicable, and/or our wealth from lawsuits or other potential hazards?
- How will future tax law changes affect my plan, and most important, my goals?

- Is it better for me to personally hold title to my assets?

- What are the various forms of ownership to consider?

- What are the potential advantages/disadvantages of each structure?

- Will some assets perform better in the short/mid/long term if they are "owned" by some sort of a trust, corporation, family partnership, or other entity?

- Will my current structure of ownership achieve my goals? (In some cases, it is better to *control* assets than to own them.)

- Do I have an up-to-date tax management plan to reduce income and capital gains taxes?

- If married, what would happen if my spouse and I split up?

- Are my investments protecting me from rising or falling interest rates?

- With regard to my assets, do I have too many eggs in one basket?

- Am I taking advantage of every helpful point of law?

- Is there anything else I can do to move closer to my goals?

- What are the most efficient ways to transfer cash or assets to my heirs?

Questions for Your Death Estate

- If married, will my spouse/family be provided for?

- If married, what would happen if my spouse and I split up?

- Does my estate plan consist of the necessary, cohesive trust(s) and a will?

- Do I know what my estate taxes would be if death occurred today, 10 years from now, or 20 years from now?

- Have I arranged for testamentary gifts so I receive tax benefits now?

- Should I limit distributions of principal over time?

- How will future tax law changes affect my plan, and most important, my goals?
- Am I satisfied that, after my death, my estate will be settled quickly and according to my desires?
- How much life insurance, if any, do I really need or want?
- Am I taking advantage of every helpful point of law?
- Is there anything else I can do to move closer to my goals?

Don't feel overwhelmed. There are a lot of questions and issues to be dealt with. Just focus on what you really, truly want to do. Then get great advisors to handle the tactical solutions and help you achieve your goals. If you're married, it is a good idea to have your spouse also go through this checklist separately and then see how your answers compare. It can be very enlightening and help move your strategic planning in a direction in which *all* goals can eventually be accomplished.

10

Financial Freedom

If you're feeling bogged down and overwhelmed in your planning process, let me tell you about a couple who won more than $70 million in a lottery. The husband and wife loved golf and were making a marginal living as golf pros. After they had won the lottery, they were asked, "What are you going to do now?" The wife responded, "Well, the first thing we're going to do is pay off all of our debts." Then the husband commented that he'd been giving some serious thought to buying his own golf course.

Most people work very hard their whole lives and never have $70 million. They try to sock away enough money in their retirement plans to be able to retire when they get to be 60 or 70 years old. Now this man wants to take his $70 million and get into the golf course business. The whole purpose of starting a business is to create a means of income for yourself sufficient to support your immediate lifestyle needs and set aside enough money for the future, or to build the equity in the business to the point where eventually you can convert the equity or investments into income so you become financially independent. So who in his right mind would take $70 million and risk it to buy a job for himself?

That is the question I asked myself when I heard about the lottery winner's response. Some people might say, "But he loves golf. It's his hobby." That's fine. I'm not criticizing his passion; I'm just wondering if his vision is too narrow. Golf may be your hobby, but that's absolutely no reason to own a golf course business. If you're worth $70 million, you could have the freedom to do what you really want to do. Money, when effectively used, represents financial

So you won the lottery? Golf may be your hobby, but that's absolutely no reason to buy a golf course business.

freedom. It's the power and freedom to go where you want, when you want, and do what you want. So, why would it make sense to take your freedom and turn it into a job?

Many people feel that they must have "something to do." It almost doesn't matter what they accomplish as long as they feel they are "doing" something. What they "do," their job, becomes a large part of their identity. Perhaps part of it stems from our childhood, from the first time we were asked, "What are you going to be when you grow up? What are you going to do?" We responded, "I'm going to be a fire fighter. I'm going to be the president. I'm going to be a banker." Often, people introduce themselves, especially at business lunches, as, "I'm so-and-so, and I'm a _____." For many people, their jobs really do define who they are. Rarely, if ever, were we asked as children, "What are you going to help the world do?"

When I heard about the lottery winners, I wondered, "If they could wave a magic wand and create the perfect situation, what would it be?" If they love golf, perhaps they would like to teach young people how to golf, provide golf scholarships, or establish a training program for people. If they have $70 million, they don't need to own the golf course in order to make those arrangements. In fact, it's probably better for them to establish arrangements with several golf courses, geographically diversified, so they can provide their scholarships, programs, training, skills and insight to more people in more places. They could be much more effective that way than owning one location at which to run their programs. They could have the freedom to go where they want and to do what they want. They could schedule their seminars, workshops or clinics all over the world. Those people could share their golf expertise. They love teaching golf and playing golf, which is entirely different from owning and managing a golf course.

The problem with a lot of people who have achieved enough equity to be financially independent is that they are so caught up in their existing jobs that they are not financially independent. "If I don't have this job, what will I do?" is an issue. A lot of people will continue to work even when they don't need to work for money or income. Why? Well, some people have the perception that if they "retire" they won't be doing anything. They don't recognize that they can be actively engaged in doing other things because they have no real sense of purpose in their lives. Their life has been defined based upon what they did for a living as opposed to what good they accomplished or what they really could be doing. You must consider what is the best use of your time, talents and resources. What is the purpose of your life?

One of my favorite examples is a fellow I met a few years ago. He was a real estate developer in his mid-80s who primarily developed condominiums. He was worth about $20 million. He was going through some aggravation trying to convert some avocado groves into condominiums. He was getting grief from the local government and the EPA. It seemed everybody was giving him a hard time about developing these avocado groves. He was introduced to me through his attorney and accountant, who said, "This guy is really frustrated by this whole thing. He's got ulcers that are acting up. He's already had a stress-related heart attack once before, and it looks as if he's on the verge of having another one."

When I talked to this fellow, he said he wasn't doing it for the money, he was doing it because of the "thrill of the hunt." I suggested to him that there were thousands of people who were capable of developing condominiums or turning avocado groves into condominium projects. It would be in his best interest, and the best interest of many others, if he found a less stressful way to apply his time, talent, energy, ability and the substantial skills that had enabled him to acquire more than $20 million in net worth. Just think of the power of teaching those skills and characteristics to other people, perhaps to inner-city youth who may not have the perspective to realize the world is bigger than the ghetto or that a person can rise up from nothing and accomplish something significant, as this gentleman had done.

I was unable to proceed with this gentleman because he died shortly after that conversation. So all the things that could have, should have, would have happened, not just in his life but in the lives of those he could have affected, all the things that he could have experienced which would have been far more fulfilling than developing condominiums, didn't happen because he was so wrapped up in what he did for a living that he totally lost sight of why he ever got a job or went to work in the first place.

Nobody goes out and gets a job because he wants to become a workaholic or to give himself an ulcer or a stress-related heart attack. Nobody sets out with those objectives, and yet many people manage to accomplish exactly that.

The irony is that too often the people in those situations don't need to be wasting away their health and their lives because they have substantial amounts of wealth. If their wealth were properly channeled, managed and structured, they would be financially independent. They would be free. And they would be able to go out into the world and make a difference, a real difference. Developing avocado groves into condominiums is not so important or unique a thing that the people involved are irreplaceable.

In the example of the golfing lottery winner, he loved golf and wanted to teach other people how to golf. That's great. Then he should teach people how to do it. But he should find a format that really makes a difference in people's lives. Find a format that really makes you free and enables you and others to become fulfilled so that you can have a positive impact on as large a cross section of people as possible. Converting financial freedom into a job is, in my opinion, inane and absolutely illogical. So is working at a job longer or harder than you have to.

So when you're setting your goals and thinking of your perfect situation, remember these examples. If you have the funds to be financially independent, remember that you can go anywhere, live anywhere and do anything. Try to remember why you started working or building your wealth in the first place. What did you want to do when you started working? What would you like to do now? What is holding you back from what you are really capable of doing and want to do?

Don't look at it as retirement. Instead, visualize replacing your existing calendar with the "perfect calendar." Let go of what is holding you back. Lovingly turn over your "job," or at least the things you don't like about your job, to someone who hasn't yet achieved enough wealth to become free. Embrace the freedom you have; begin living and enjoying your perfect calendar.

11

Procrastination = Opportunity Lost

After reading the last several chapters, you should be starting to have an idea of where you want to go and what you want to do. Once we know where we want to go, it is important to know how to get there. We need to develop our own agenda. An effective definition of this term for practical purposes is this: an agenda is a plan to carry out or further one's goals.

Everyone has an agenda, although we often hear people deny this truth. Sometimes it's hard to recognize someone else's agenda, let alone our own. It is crucial to our personal success to gain a clear picture of what is in our personal interest and what is driving those around us. This can be very difficult because there are so many components to establishing or recognizing an agenda. People who honestly don't feel they have an agenda aren't likely to have a clear picture of their business or personal goals. Therefore, they don't have a purposeful plan to accomplish that which they truly want to achieve. Simply stated, if you don't know where you're going, it doesn't matter if you get there.

Mary had been widowed for nearly 10 years. When asked if she had an agenda, she said she didn't have any particular agenda and felt that too many people did. She believed that the world was full of people only looking out for themselves. Mary had been prompted many times by her advisors to set up at least a will or a living trust. One advisor suggested that she might apply certain techniques to reduce her income taxes, benefit her children and provide funding for the hospice that had so wonderfully helped her ailing husband.

Mary said it all seemed complicated and too confusing. "I'll just think on it a bit," she would say. Her advisors would mention ideas to Mary from time to time, but her response was always the same, "I'll just think on it a bit." Well, she thought about it for 10 years, but she *did* nothing. When she died, her children lost $5 million in estate taxes. That's $5 million Congress got to spend any way it wanted. The hospice where Mary volunteered more than 20 hours each week got nothing.

Would Mary have been happy about this? Mary loved her children and felt strongly about the good work the hospice did. Did Mary believe Congress would be a good steward of her $5 million? No. Mary often commented on how "that arrogant Congress and government bureaucracy" abused her income taxes. The $70,000 or so she paid in annual income tax pales by comparison to the $5 million lost in estate tax. The hospice will miss the $50,000 annual contribution Mary made each year, but it will sorely miss the millions of dollars it could have received if she had identified her goals, developed her agenda and carried out her plan.

She had goals, even if she didn't consciously recognize them. She wanted to leave an inheritance for her children. She wanted to avoid giving unnecessary money to the government. She wanted to help the hospice. She just hadn't developed a plan or agenda to carry out those goals. She died with good intentions, but no documentation or action to realize her goals.

Mary thought too many people had agendas. I believe the world is full of too many people who lack a personal agenda. In Mary's case, it cost her a lot. It cost her a legacy. Her community and her heirs lost out. It also cost her the fulfillment and happiness she might have enjoyed while alive. It cost her the peace of mind of knowing that she had a multifaceted agenda that would benefit others. Mary had not taken an honest approach to her own needs on the philosophical level. She mistakenly felt that to have an agenda would make her self-serving or somehow dishonest. Having an established, properly executed agenda actually enables you to achieve your goals and, in most cases, benefit others in the process.

We are at our best, our very happiest, when our agenda, our lives and resources have a positive effect on others. The more people or causes enhanced by our agenda, the happier and more fulfilled we become. An agenda that places an individual at the center of the universe will not make that person happy or effective in the long run. This, of course, is because we as individuals are not the object around which all else revolves, despite what we sometimes think.

So once we have identified our goals and recognized that we need to establish a personal agenda, we are ready to begin implementing strategies to fulfill those goals.

12

Vision, Goals, Strategies, Tactics, Tools and Timing

Countless times every day in America and all around the world, an investor begins a discussion with an investment advisor to discuss the possibilities of investing new money or rethinking existing investments. The advisor will typically ask, "What are your goals for this investment?" The client will respond with something like, "I want this investment to grow," "I want this investment to produce income," or "I want to make this investment so that it can grow and eventually be used to pay for college tuition for my child (or my grandchild, nephew or niece)." This is how many investors describe their goals. And when an investor isn't sure how to answer the question, the advisor will usually offer as examples similar phrases in an attempt to define goals.

Unfortunately, the entire dialogue is dysfunctional and misguided.

Most investment advisors, attorneys, accountants, insurance advisors and financial planners cannot accurately describe the differences between goals, strategies, tactics and tools, nor describe the role of timing in the far-reaching needs of the client's life. There are distinct differences between goals and strategies and tactics. A goal is the desired end result or our vision of what our lives are all about. The strategies and tactics are the means used to achieve the goals. In this chapter, we will further explore the true definitions of these terms and their significance so that consumers and professionals can share a clear view of each topic and how they apply in given circumstances.

Goals relate to your lifestyle. One common goal could be stated as, "I want to live the perfect calendar. I want to spend my time, talents and resources doing this list of things." Other goals could include statements like, "I want to provide for my spouse when I die, or if my spouse predeceases me, I would like to be adequately provided for." Other goals could include, "I would like to pay for some or all of the college expenses for this individual or this group of individuals." An example of a philanthropic goal would be, "I would like to endow these causes." These are all goals. Investing for growth is not a goal. Investing for income is not a goal. Reducing taxes is not a goal. Those are all strategies, not goals.

Key strategies fall into the following categories:

1. **Growth** — The desire to accumulate the magic number; i.e., how much is enough?

2. **Income** — The amount of cash flow you need to support your preferred lifestyle.

3. **Exit or Transition** — The method used to move yourself to the next level. This is a relevant strategy at many times during one's life, especially when thinking macro or transformational as opposed to micro or transactional.

4. **Distribution** — How your wealth will be distributed:

   A. During your lifetime

   B. After your death

5. **Legal Liability and Tax Avoidance** — How to keep your wealth once you've earned it.

Timing is a critical factor in each of these categories. We will explore timing later in this chapter.

When a conversation between a client and a professional advisor, be it an attorney, accountant, stock broker, financial advisor, investment advisor, financial planner, real estate agent or banker, is allowed to progress without a clear understanding of how all of these topics play a role in managing the client's wealth, the outcome can only be confused and the relationship frustrated. You can imagine how difficult it is when a client states, for example, that his goal is to have a consulting agreement with the company he's selling so that he can continue to put $100,000 a year away in his qualified plan. Putting money in a qualified plan is never a goal. It is a tactic. Unfortunately, however, many advisors will not stop their clients in their incorrect thinking and educate the clients as to what goals really are. And so the confusion persists. The ultimate result is reflected in the financial chaos most people experience.

Tactics, by definition in strategic planning, are those things which we employ in order to fulfill a particular strategy. As an example, if your strategy is to maximize and grow your net worth and a qualified plan is available to you, then a viable tactic might be some type of qualified plan. Other tactics would be structural entities such as family limited partnerships, limited liability companies, trusts and so on. So tactics are, by definition, ways to hold title which provide benefits, especially those that will most efficiently fulfill your strategy and, ultimately, fulfill your goals.

Tools in strategic planning are items such as real estate, stocks, bonds, CDs, annuities, mutual funds, professionally managed accounts, life insurance, disability insurance, health insurance, liability insurance, etc. Tools are actual products used to fund or capitalize a strategy to achieve a goal.

Many professionals are confused about what role they should play in macro strategic planning. For example, most lawyers, accountants, fee-based financial planners and other people who render advice on a fee basis rather than a commission basis, tend to be focusing on tactics. Their primary emphasis lies in which tactics can be implemented since their compensation is derived from rendering tactical advice and/or by implementing tactics. However, one could argue that lawyers cross over into the tools business because their compensation is often derived from the creation of actual documents; therefore, the entity created by those documents could possibly be viewed as a tool, product or even commodity.

The tools-oriented professionals tend to be compensated as a result of the sale or promotion of a product such as stocks, bonds, mutual funds, insurance products and real estate. By and large we can discover what the true nature of a professional's business is by looking at how he or she is compensated.

As consumers, we must be sure we are not confused about the distinction between goals, strategies, tactics and tools, because wherever there is confusion, there is the potential for disaster. A necessary component of being "on the right page" with our advisors is making sure we are speaking the same language, we are familiar with the terminology, and we all understand what the game really is. Trouble often occurs when advisors who are not adequately trained in the true nature of goalsetting confuse the process and immediately jump into the tools mode or tactics mode. Directly stated, some "advisors" are actually salespeople who jump into the sales role as soon as possible.

My firm sees the evidence of this confusion all the time as we review estate planning documents, insurance contracts and investments. The clients generally aren't sure what they have or why they have it. There is no entrance, growth and exit strategy with each of their assets. As an example, a client could have hundreds of thousands or even many millions of dollars in stock or real estate and not be able to provide an accurate outline of why it was purchased, when it was purchased, at what price it was purchased and what the holding period of the asset should be. Basically, the asset was purchased because the client hoped it was going to go up in value. And it did. But the client didn't determine what to do with it after it reached a certain value. There's no discipline to know when to transition out. We often see people in their 70s and 80s who own assets suited to someone who is trying to build or create a large amount of personal wealth but very unsuited to someone who is looking into distribution strategies or tactics.

Only *after* defining our goals should we explore the various strategies and tactics available to fulfill our goals. Simply put, a growth strategy helps your net worth grow; an income strategy maximizes your income; and a distribution strategy deals with how your wealth will be distributed. To carry out each strategy, a variety of tactics can be appropriately employed, such as trusts, gifts, IRAs, 401(k)s and donations. With the help of expert advisors, we want to implement strategies that will empower us to accomplish our life's vision, mission and objectives, not hinder us from achieving fulfillment. We cannot begin to outline a plan or set of strategies for my firm's clients until we discover and confirm their goals and needs.

Some of the most frequent inquiries my firm addresses have to do with investment selection. Since my firm is not engaged in the sale or delivery of investment services, insurance or annuity products, we do not provide specific advice on these issues. What we do offer is important conceptual enlightenment as well as individual, specific insight as to action plans which capitalize upon and maximize one's total wealth.

Because the financial world is constantly changing, I cannot offer specific or individual analysis. However, the following analogy illustrates what should be a timeless and universal view of financial tactics, strategy and implementation. Think of it as building a custom home:

Step 1: Vision and Goals

The first thing you need to build your dream house is a vision: location (anywhere in the world), style of architecture, floor plan, etc. Next you set specific goals, such as amount of square footage, number of bedrooms and bathrooms, number of levels and so on. You might be able to do this on your own, or you might bring in an expert early on to help you realize all the options available. If you could wave a magic wand, what would your perfect home be like?

Step 2: Strategic Plan

Once the details of your vision are documented in writing, you will want to develop a macro strategic plan to get from where you are now to what you want in the future. This strategic plan must be put in writing. Once double checked for flaws and determined to be complete, this document must be implemented as the blueprint or plan. This plan outlines the specific tactics and timeline which will take you through each phase of development. It is critical to note that it is the overall plan which must dominate the tactics. Please understand that tactics and tools must be temporary and disposable. They are merely the means to execute the plan and fulfill the goals or vision.

Step 3: Tactics and Tools

Before you can begin work on the foundation of your house, you realize you must first prepare the land. You decide whether you want the land flat or multilevel based upon your plan. You employ a tool called a bulldozer to prepare the land. Once you get the land in shape, you stop using the bulldozer. The bulldozer has a limited tactical life in the execution of your plan. *Warning*: Do not attempt to use the bulldozer to pour the foundation, cut the lumber, frame the house, install the plumbing or electrical work, and most important, don't try to use a bulldozer to install the roof!

If you think this example is ridiculous, just consider your own asset mix or portfolio. If your goal is to grow your estate for your own needs, do you have investments more suitable to a retirement income plan; i.e., corporate bonds, CDs, municipal bonds, trust deeds? If your goal is to maximize income for yourself or your heirs, why do you have growth-oriented assets in your portfolio? If your estate is above the federal estate tax exemption or unified credit, why are you holding title in your own name or living trust when other options may be vastly superior?

Implements such as bulldozers can be of great help in the tactical execution of *part* of your plan. So can stocks, bonds, annuities, CDs, insurance policies, living trusts, family partnerships, limited liability companies or corporations, etc. Just as you recognize the lunacy of using bulldozers to install a roof, you must learn to recognize the proper applications and limitations of other tactics and tools.

There is an old Russian proverb with universal application: "To a man with a hammer, the whole world is a nail." It is critical that we remain focused on our goals and not the tools or tactics we are using to reach those goals. We must not become so attached to some inanimate and disposable tool, tactic, investment, etc., that we impede our own goals. Tactics or tools do indeed have a limited period of usefulness. We must recognize this and act accordingly.

I do not expect, nor do I recommend, that you establish your own set of strategies. What I do advocate is that you meet with a skilled, expert group of advisors, work with them to discover your goals, and let them help you determine which strategies, tactics and tools are best for you.

An accountant offered the following story about how poor timing combined with a lack of vision cost his own family and friends financial independence. The CPA's wife and two of her friends started a software development company in their spare bedrooms. They quickly moved into the big time and in less than a year, their little development company was worth a lot of money. They had over 200 employees and phenomenal growth.

The accountant, serving as part-time CFO, made sure the company was protected from disaster in that all proper papers were in place: business continuation documents, key person insurance, liability measures and insurance, etc. Each of the major shareholders had "complete estate plans" and their own teams of personal attorneys, accountants, insurance agents, bankers and investment advisors. They were multimillionaires, wealthy enough to be financially independent. Everyone worked long, hard hours. Often they would joke about how they could sell some or all of their massively appreciated stock and "live the good life."

Naturally, some competitors came along and introduced a better, faster, slicker product. In less than six months, the stock price fell from $12 per share to 75 cents per share. The accountant and his partners had employed every "reasonable and customary measure" to manage and protect the business and their personal wealth. But sometimes working hard and long isn't enough and "reasonable and customary measures" are inadequate. They represent the cart with square wheels or "inside the box" thinking. The company was founded on an innovative idea. But management failed to continue innovating. Someone else came along and redefined the market. The old technology couldn't compete in the new market.

Each of the shareholders of the accountant's company went from financial independence to working class stiff because neither they nor their advisors thought or operated "outside the box." They lacked innovative vision for their business market, but most important, they lacked a macro approach to seeing and capturing the personal wealth they had created. These people had hired personal and corporate advisors and business consultants and paid hundreds of thousands of dollars in fees for "reasonable and customary measures." What they needed, professionally and personally, was vision. In the left-brain analysis, they did just about everything correctly. When it came to right-brain vision, they had none.

For more insight on how to avoid this type of corporate or business tragedy, please read or listen to *Only the Paranoid Survive*, by Andrew Grove. As the CEO of Intel, he has been through these business dilemmas and has overcome the stumbling blocks that lead to so many disasters.

One cannot underestimate the critical importance of vision and timing. You and your advisors must recognize that vision and timing are crucial on a macro strategic planning level as well as in the micro day-to-day management of any number of business and personal issues. It is important that we realize how much is enough and when it is enough, so that our advisory team can apply the necessary discipline to get us out of the day-to-day grind. Mr. Grove's observation that a certain amount of paranoia is essential to success in business is right on target. I must add that it is also crucial to each of us personally. The markets are beyond our personal influence, but we can always control our own behavior and action. Please do not underestimate the value of perspective or vision. Lacking the right perspective, many people fail to see and capture the real fruit of their labors, which is freedom. If you ask your advisors whether you've exhausted all of the reasonable and customary measures for managing your finances or your business and they say yes, please remember this example. Far too often the reasonable and customary measures amount to just too little, too late. Sound vision demands "outside the box" perspective.

13

Micro Tactical Planning

Dreams do not become reality by themselves. The realization of your dreams is only possible if you work with an expert team of advisors who can provide timely implementation, persistence, intricate execution of details, diligence and focus. Without appropriate attention to detail, commitment to your plan and discipline and courage in execution, you will lose. If we define winning as the achievement of the goals in the macro strategic plan, then losing ought not to be an option.

Once a macro strategic plan has been developed and is adopted by the client and all relevant advisors, it is time to implement the strategies, tactics and timeline to achieve the goals. The micro tactical plan provides those details. It is not enough to have a great macro strategic plan; you must have the micro tactical plan to realize the benefits or desired outcomes described in your macro strategic plan.

If you really want to achieve the highest quality of life, you will need a great team. Anything less than a great team will produce less than great results. Please do not sabotage yourself by working with sub-par advisors. And don't be your own worst enemy. Do not behave as a moving target. Once the macro and micro plans are as they should be, commit yourself to fulfillment. Do not get in your own way or in the way of your team. Exercise the requisite courage to change those things that must change.

Your level of commitment and your advisors' technical and cognitive abilities are directly related to the achievement of your goals. It's up to you to choose how committed and how focused you will be. It's up to you to choose how capable and committed each member of your team will be. After all is said and done, your future is up to you.

Micro Tactical Management

Your micro tactical plan needs to be broken down into key components composed of tactics, tools and timing issues. In order to make this clear to your existing and future advisors, each macro goal should be identified then followed by the micro tactical plan, or details, as in the two following samples.

The following are just rough sketches so you can see what a micro tactical plan looks like. *Please keep in mind that these examples are for illustrative purposes only.* The recommendations are highly condensed and very incomplete. (In other words, do not structure your personal situation based upon these examples.) The first example takes a look at a small portion of a plan for a couple who have yet to obtain their magic number or enough equity to be financially independent. The second is a snapshot of a plan created for a couple who have already exceeded their magic number but needed a change in direction in order to achieve more fulfilling lives.

Example #1: A couple who have yet to achieve their magic number

Macro Goals

A. In order to achieve true financial independence, you have indicated that you will need to build an investment portfolio of $4 million to produce your desired annual income without diluting your portfolio principal. Once properly invested in a truly diversified, low-risk, income-oriented portfolio earning 5% net after taxes, you will receive $200,000 of net annual income.

B. You desire a debt-free existence. You want to own two residences valued at $1.5 million in Arizona and $2.2 million in Colorado. Furnishings, automobiles and other miscellaneous belongings will total $450,000.

C. In case of personal, family or other crisis, you have indicated that $200,000 separate from your investment capital will be sufficient to satisfy your emergency and security needs.

D. To take advantage of future business investments in either your own ideas or the attractive ideas of others, you want an additional $1.5 million of venture capital.

In the interest of space, the remaining goals have not been illustrated and only one micro strategic planning tactic has been included.

Micro Facilitation

In order to achieve your desired net worth of $9.65 million, you will need to completely rethink your approach to the wealth building process. With your current system and the savings and growth assumptions you provided, you will only achieve a net worth of $1.7 million within 23 years, or by age 52. Therefore, we suggest that you reposition yourself into a career where you achieve the following:

1. Earn enough excess income to set aside at least $135,000, hopefully more, each year in diversified growth investments. Ideally, you will want to earn an average of 20% per year appreciation. Additionally, you should also take full advantage of any tax deferred qualified plans such as 401(k)s, pensions or profit sharing plans.

2. Either start a business or begin working for a company in which you can accumulate a large amount of stock. You will need both income and equity for your labors. Furthermore, you must start or work for a company with an eye towards growth, expansion and with an exit strategy congruent with the owners' (shareholders') goals. This is what we refer to as an entrance, growth and exit strategy.

In the interest of space, other recommendations have been left out.

Achieving the second couple's perfect calendar required many changes in strategy, tactics and tools. A sample timeline is included to demonstrate when tactics should be implemented and the outcome with respect to meeting certain goals.

Example #2: A couple who have exceeded their magic number

Macro Goal

Income of $300,000 annually net after taxes, sufficient to support the desired lifestyle. This income is to come solely from investment capital, so that you can live your perfect calendar and not have to generate income from your activities. You are ready to exchange your job and ownership of ABC Inc. for your perfect calendar.

Micro Facilitation

Your current net after tax income from investments is approximately $170,000. To achieve your desired income of $300,000 net after taxes from investment capital rather than a job, you should do the following:

1 . Convert the assets most suitable for exchange or conversion, especially your company ABC Inc., from their current status into more appropriate positions for income generation. (Please see section "Investment Policy" provided by __(advisor)__ for complete details.)

2.   The following assets have been identified by mutual agreement between you and __(advisor)__ for conversion:

Asset	Market Value	Cost Basis	Debt	Annual Income
A. Agricultural Land	$500,000	$118,000	$0	$15,000
B. 2650 Bridle Path	$875,000	$200,000	$0	$22,000
C. Intel Stock	$800,000	$100,000	$0	$10,000
D. CLO Stock	$1,900,000	$25,000	$0	$10,000
E. ABC Stock	$3,400,000	$150,000	$0	$0
F. Personal Use	$3,700,000		$0	$0
Total	$11,175,000	$0	$0	$57,000

3. Now that these assets have been selected for conversion, you should transfer them from their existing title to the proposed title *prior* to conversion.

Asset	Current Title	New Title
A. Agricultural Land	Living Trust	FLP
B. 2650 Bridle Path	Living Trust	FLP
C. Intel Stock	Living Trust	CRT
D. CLO Stock	Living Trust	CRT
E. ABC Stock	Living Trust	CRT

In order to effect this transition, you must first create the entity(s) which will be used to hold title as desired for the future. Your attorney has provided you with the customized documents necessary to establish the desired entity(s) along with the necessary documents to transfer title. (Appendix includes legal/tactical description of entity(s). The copies of legal documents are found in the document section of your plan.) The following illustration demonstrates the recommended title changes and the impact of converting your assets into a portfolio more suitable for your goals.

Annual

Asset	Market Value	Cost Basis	Debt	Title	After Tax
A. Income Portfolio	$6,100,000	N/A	0	CRT	$305,000
B. Emergency Fund	$200,000	$200,000	0	Living Trust	$8,500
C. Growth Investments	$1,375,000	$225,000	0	FLP	$32,000
D. Personal Use	$3,700,000	$1,600,000	0	Living Trust	$0
Totals	**$11,375,000**				**$345,500**

Timing

To complete this portion of your plan, you should follow this timeline:

October	November	December
Implement CRT. Transfer title of assets to CRT. Convert trust assets as proposed by advisor in your written investment policy.	Begin earning interest on the assets transferred to and then converted in your CRT.	Continue earning increased income on CRT assets.

January	April	July
Receive first quarterly income distribution from CRT. Enjoy increased income.	Receive second quarterly income distribution. Enjoy increased income.	Receive third quarterly income distribution. Enjoy increased income.

I hope that even in this greatly abbreviated form you have found these samples helpful in strengthening your understanding of how critical a role micro tactical planning plays in the achievement of goals. People often ask me why their existing advisors have not addressed their macro and micro issues in an understandable and articulate format. They want to know why it is that after spending thousands, even tens of thousands, of dollars they still don't know where they are or how they are really doing overall. Why do so many people live in a state of financial chaos? By the time you finish this book, I believe that if you really want to know the answers to these questions, you will have found them.

III

Wealth:
How to Manage It —
Selecting Advisors

14

Your All-Star Team

What is the best way to select advisors to help us achieve our goals?

Sometimes people take upon themselves tasks and projects of absolutely tremendous importance even though they are among the very least qualified people on the face of the planet to engage in those particular tasks. Sometimes they have the attitude that because they are successful at ranching, business, or whatever their backgrounds may be, they are automatically going to be successful in managing their wealth. What delusions the human ego can contrive!

In order for people to benefit from the advice and counsel of a professional, they must recognize that they need help. This can be a very difficult adjustment for some people, especially for successful people. Some amateur athletes try to coach themselves instead of seeking professional help, but you'll notice that the professional athletes who are most successful have had a great deal of coaching from various high-level, well-respected teachers. This is absolutely essential for superior performance.

In advanced wealth management, some people try to coach themselves. Yet most of these people would not be hired by anyone else to do advanced wealth management or macro strategic planning. Furthermore, they wouldn't hire themselves if they stepped back and looked at the situation. They think, "I'm going to study this out myself. I'm smart enough and intelligent enough to figure it out." They fail to ask themselves, "Am I really so good at these things that anyone else would hire me? Would someone looking for really good advisors hire me? If I put myself in the marketplace as a financial guru, would anybody hire me?" If the answer is no, then what the heck are they doing making decisions entirely on their own, doing their own research and performing their own analysis? Part of the challenge when selecting advisors is to discern who is truly knowledgeable, experienced and expert in a given area versus who is marginally competent. On important issues, we need advisors who are in the highest echelon of competency.

So, rule number one in selecting advisors is to know when to fire yourself.

Even the most independent, self-reliant, self-made person should be able to realize that the strategies, tactics, tools and timing involved in achieving financial goals are complicated and require the interdependent use of expert advisors. Unfortunately, we are not each blessed with an all-knowing guru who sits on a rock, waiting to dispense the keys to our success. If we look for such a person, we will soon discover that no one mortal can provide us with all of the wisdom, experience and intuition needed to make all the right decisions all the time, or even most of the time. Therefore, we need multiple advisors with a variety of backgrounds, experience, training and, very important, long-standing records of success and a view toward innovative thinking and vision.

In our complex society, no one professional advisor can keep abreast of the rapidly growing body of information on wealth management issues. We live in an interdependent world. We need a team of expert advisors. Think of yourself as the manager of a basketball team. Of the millions of people who can dribble a basketball, only a few qualify as professional all-stars. The all-stars achieve the best results. They are the best basketball players. *You get to pick your very own all-star team of advisors out of the numerous advisors available.* When all is said and done, it is the quality, competency and creativity of the advisors you select that largely determines your success.

One tool that can be of enormous help in selecting great advisors as well as determining your own level of knowledge is a rating system. In order to help you truly understand the points in this chapter, I've included this exercise. It needs to be experienced in two parts. Please do not cheat yourself by skipping ahead.

Rate Your Knowledge — Phase One

On a scale of 0-10, please rate your level of expertise. A rating of zero would indicate that you have never heard of the subject before. A rating of 10 would indicate that you are one of the top 25 people in the country on that respective subject.

0-10

_____ The rollover and reinvestment of qualified plan assets

_____ Avoiding the triple or quadruple tax on qualified plans

_____ Irrevocable Life Insurance Trust design and funding

_____ Specific advanced strategies that provide living benefits vs. inheritance benefits

_____ 1035 Exchanges

_____ Rule 144 stock transactions

_____ 1036 Exchanges

_____ Mergers and acquisitions

_____ 664 Exchanges

_____ The formation and administration of Asset Protection Trusts and various offshore strategies

_____ Current Income, Capital Gains and Estate Tax rates, deductions and exclusions

_____ Proposed or recent changes to the tax rates, deductions or exclusions

_____ Multigenerational planning

_____ Generation Skipping Trust parameters and planning techniques

_____ The limitations, disadvantages and advantages of Living Trusts

_____ Social Security rules, regulations and procedures

_____ Medicare rules, regulations and procedures

_____ The use of Tax-Exempt Trusts to sell highly appreciated assets without capital gains taxes

_____ Business Macro Strategic Planning

_____ Limited Liability Companies

_____ Family Limited Partnerships

_____ Grantor Retained Income Trusts (GRITs)

_____ Grantor Retained Annuity Trusts (GRATs)

_____ Grantor Retained Unitrusts (GRUTs)

_____ Qualified Personal Residence Trusts (QPRTs)

_____ Self Canceling Installment Notes (SCINs)

_____ Personal and/or Family Macro Strategic Planning

_____ Private Family Foundations, Supporting Foundations/ Organizations

_____ Gifting & Freezing strategies

_____ Trustee, Custodial and Administrative services

_____ Tax filing, tax projections and related accounting services

_____ Income, Capital Gains and Estate Tax reduction and elimination tactics

_____ Risk reduction through diversification

_____ Financing arrangements for business and personal needs

_____ Real estate sales and exchanges (1031)

_____ Fulfilling philanthropic desires through charitable planning

_____ Goal identification and problem recognition techniques

_____ Growth investment selection and ongoing portfolio timing and management

_____ Income investment selection and ongoing portfolio timing and management

_____ Paradigm recognition and shifting techniques

When I first introduced "Rate Your Knowledge," it only consisted of Phase One. Right away I learned that we would have to introduce a more "structured" rating system. Many who completed the exercise had a tendency to at least slightly overrate their level of knowledge. Some people, especially the very successful, professional advisors, actually rated themselves at levels exceeding 10. One person went so far as to rate himself as a level 15 on a couple of topics.

One of the key problem areas for the entire financial services industry is that there is no quantifiable rating system to clarify one's level of competency. Most of the industry looks to production of revenue or amount of product sold to gauge effectiveness or competency. This is a major stumbling block. While the ability to generate revenue can offer some indication of ability, other factors must also be taken into consideration. Most of us can think of at least one professional—attorney, investment advisor/ broker, accountant, banker, insurance agent, financial planner or real estate agent—who thinks he or she is brilliant in the field and who bases this perception upon their level of personal income or accomplishment in sales. Organizations or industries that equate production with brilliance are ultimately hurting everyone involved.

The ability to sell products or generate billable hours must not be considered the most important factor in determining competency. Yet as a general rule, recognition throughout the financial services industry is based upon sales or revenue. As the public becomes more sophisticated, it becomes more wary, more interested in substance and less interested in hype. Many consumers have already had personal experiences with the super salesman types who have sold them on ineffective, piecemeal solutions such as living trusts, qualified plans or life insurance which do not fully meet their macro needs. Just how many people do you suppose have lost money on limited partnerships or other investments that didn't perform as promoted? Such consumer experiences combined with today's flood of information will have a detrimental effect upon those salespeople who rely upon their own charm and "salesmanship" to gain business.

As people become more sophisticated, they demand higher levels of competence from their advisors. Professionals who want to participate in the businesses, finances and activities of A- level clients must hold themselves to a higher standard. Phase Two of "Rate Your Knowledge" has been designed with all this in mind. The difference between phases one and two is of enormous consequence. Phase Two incorporates into the rating system a reasonable set of competency standards. Those who might be tempted to exaggerate their abilities or expertise must be careful now.

With a rating of 4 or above, it becomes easy for professionals and/or consumers to verify expertise. Note that no credit is given for salesmanship, chairman's club awards, etc. The rating system for performance standards is based, as it should be, solely on: A) your level of knowledge on a subject, and B) your ability to perform in the client's best interest. You cannot be rated a level 7 or better without your clients, peers and competitors recognizing you as an authority on the subject. Just as important, if you are not client-centered, your peers will know. Self-centered or profit-centered individuals would not likely gain long-term client and peer respect, thus preventing them from attaining level 7 or higher.

Once we know where we are, we can make enormous progress, if we choose to. One investment advisor/branch manager friend of mine went to a meeting for all of his firm's branch managers. His peers voted him the "most technically knowledgeable" branch manager in that firm. When I met him, he rated level 6 in a few topics and mostly zero, 1 or 2 on everything else. I asked him how much time he had spent studying to become the "most technically knowledgeable" manager in the firm. He answered that he had invested approximately 20 hours of reading and studying to pull himself up to level 3 or 4 on many topics. He figured that in another 40 to 50 hours he would reach level 3 or 4 on everything. He now felt confident that level 7 or better was achievable in core business areas.

Ask yourself: If you or a family member were about to have surgery, what minimum level of competency would you want the surgeon and his support team to possess? Now if you were going to select a team of financial advisors, what minimum level of competency would you insist that they possess? What kind of advisors do *you* want surrounding *you*?

By completing Phase Two of this exercise, you will have a better understanding of your strengths, weaknesses and core competency or that of your advisors.

Rate Your Knowledge — Phase Two

Please rate your knowledge of the following subject areas using the scale below.

0 = You have never heard of the subject.

1 = You have at least heard of the subject before.

2 = You have a vague understanding of the subject.

3 = You have been involved in some meaningful exploration of the subject.

4 = You could provide a reasonably accurate verbal or written summary of the subject.

5 = You could provide a very accurate verbal or written summary of the subject.

6 = You have firsthand personal and/or professional experience with the subject.

7 = You are considered by many of your peers to be the best local authority on the subject.

8 = You are highly compensated for your work in the area. Peers, friends and even competitors recognize you as being an expert in the top 5% of your field.

9 = You are highly compensated for your work in the area. Peers, friends and even competitors recognize you as being in the top 5% in your field, *and* not only do you have technical ability, but your total breadth of knowledge and creative ability empower you to apply your skills in a macro sense.

10 = You are considered to be an international authority and/or you are in the top 1% in your field or niche.

11 = There are no elevens.

0-10

_____ The rollover and reinvestment of qualified plan assets

_____ Avoiding the triple or quadruple tax on qualified plans

_____ Irrevocable Life Insurance Trust design and funding

_____ Specific advanced strategies that provide living benefits vs. inheritance benefits

_____ 1035 Exchanges

_____ Rule 144 stock transactions

_____ 1036 Exchanges

_____ Mergers and acquisitions

_____ 664 Exchanges

_____ The formation and administration of Asset Protection Trusts and various offshore strategies

_____ Current Income, Capital Gains and Estate Tax rates, deductions and exclusions

_____ Proposed or recent changes to the tax rates, deductions or exclusions

_____ Multigenerational planning

_____ Generation Skipping Trust parameters and planning techniques

_____ The limitations, disadvantages and advantages of Living Trusts

_____ Social Security rules, regulations and procedures

_____ Medicare rules, regulations and procedures

_____ The use of Tax-Exempt Trusts to sell highly appreciated assets without capital gains taxes

_____ Business Macro Strategic Planning

_____ Limited Liability Companies

_____ Family Limited Partnerships

_____ Grantor Retained Income Trusts (GRITs)

_____ Grantor Retained Annuity Trusts (GRATs)

_____ Grantor Retained Unitrusts (GRUTs)

_____ Qualified Personal Residence Trusts (QPRTs)

_____ Self Canceling Installment Notes (SCINs)

_____ Personal and/or Family Macro Strategic Planning

_____ Private Family Foundations, Supporting Foundations

_____ Gifting & Freezing strategies

_____ Trustee, Custodial and Administrative services

_____ Tax filing, tax projections and related accounting services

_____ Income, Capital Gains and Estate Tax reduction and elimination tactics

_____ Risk reduction through diversification

_____ Financing arrangements for business and personal needs

_____ Real estate sales and exchanges (1031)

_____ Fulfilling philanthropic desires through charitable planning

_____ Goal identification and problem recognition techniques

_____ Growth investment selection and ongoing portfolio timing and management

_____ Income investment selection and ongoing portfolio timing and management

_____ Paradigm recognition and shifting techniques

Besides having the knowledge and experience of our advisors to help us, we must also consider the agendas of the advisors on our team. We need to make sure their goals are in harmony with ours, lest their greed or self-interest interfere with the achievement of our objectives. On the other hand, we need to be certain that our own self-interest or arrogance doesn't interfere with our ability to retain a quality team. We and our advisors must have the attitude, "We're in this together." We need a system where everybody puts into and takes out of the relationship in an equitable, although not necessarily equal, manner. Any relationship that benefits one side disproportionately will eventually fail. Real trust and rapport can only be established in mutually beneficial scenarios.

Some might argue that the client-advisor relationship is not important because advisors or clients are "a dime a dozen." What leaps to my mind is a term from the financial industry, "churn and burn." This refers to the practice of using a client to make a sale and not worrying about the long-term effect on the client or the client-advisor relationship. Some clients also behave in a "churn and burn" mode, burning through a long list of advisors, believing that new advisors are just a phone call away and that the relationship is not important. Such attitudes are delusionary and, in my experience, have proven disastrous every time, without exception. It is possible to take unfair advantage of another person for some limited period of time, but just as the financial markets and indices are interconnected, so is everything in life. Experience proves that what goes around eventually comes around, sometimes with momentum.

Integrity is a key component in any successful long-term relationship. We should only do business with people of impeccable integrity, whether we are client or advisor. Simply stated, if people do not conduct themselves and their business with integrity, they are not worth the risk of our time, talent or resources. Of course, part of the challenge is this: The advisors with the most exciting ideas are often the most suspect. On the other side of the coin, the prospective new client, "Mr. and Mrs. Big Bucks," may be looking to fleece the advisor of any and all ideas as well as his or her time without fair compensation. Things just work better if all the players in the relationship are centered in integrity and willing to listen to the truth, tell the truth and act upon the truth.

Is it possible to find good advisors? Yes. Are there traps to watch out for and avoid? Absolutely. How many times have we heard, "It's all my broker's (banker's, attorney's, accountant's, real estate agent's, etc.) fault. If I hadn't followed that clown's advice, this never would have happened"? We may even have had these feelings ourselves. However, here's that often painful dose of medicine called reality: None of these feelings, excuses, or responsibility shifts really matter. Remember, after all the blaming is done, our net worth is what it is. No more, no less. That's the reality we have to live with.

But how can we tell whether or not the people we've selected are providing us with all the expertise we need? Are we really getting the best advice possible? Are our existing advisors really doing a thorough job? Are we hearing about all of the options available?

Some people become very quickly enamored of professionals who sound impressive. You have to ask yourself if they sound good to you because they are telling you what

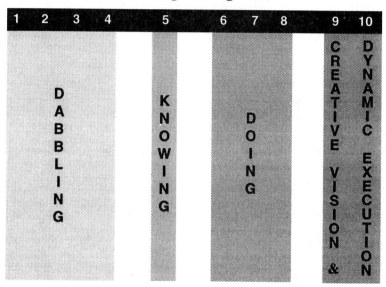

you want to hear or because they are highly regarded within their profession for having a high level of experience, precision, knowledge and competence.

The chart below is one I often use when teaching or consulting with professionals and consumers in person.

Knowledge Rating Scale

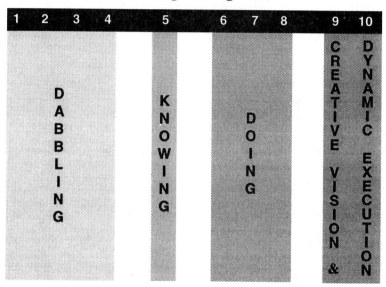

Interpreting Knowledge/Experience Levels

Levels 0-4 = Dabbling
> Never trust anything to a dabbler.

Level 5 = Knowing
> Knowledge is a good thing. Knowledge alone, however, is insufficient.

Levels 6-8 = Doing
> Knowledge combined with experience is where competent representation begins.

Levels 9-10 = Creative Vision and Dynamic Execution
> Welcome to the A-level game. Levels 9 and 10 are where art and science are masterfully combined.

Part of selecting good advisors is being able to take our ego and emotions out of the process. A lot of advisors who want to do business with us are going to attempt to get that business by telling us what we want to hear and, in effect, pandering to our egos and making us feel good about ourselves. Sometimes what we really need is for somebody to hit us between the eyes with a two-by-four called the truth and tell us that we might be acting as our own worst enemy.

Unfortunately, there's no guarantee that the advisors we pick are going to do the best job for us. But there are ways we can effectively weed out those who won't and give ourselves a better chance at picking those who will. Below are some guidelines for choosing advisors. We'll discuss these points further in the following chapters.

- *Congruent Agendas*: Recognize your advisors' agendas by asking, "What's in it for them?" Make sure their agendas are in alignment with yours. There is nothing wrong with advisors wanting to provide for themselves and their families, but make sure their self-interest doesn't override the benefit to you.

- *Don't Deal With Dabblers*: No one person can expertly handle all the complex strategies needed to manage your wealth. When something as important as your personal or family security or wealth is involved, get the best help available. Would you rather have a general practitioner or a neurosurgeon performing your brain surgery?

- *Check Referrals*: Advisor candidates will only provide you with good referrals. Besides talking to satisfied clients, check to see if the advisor is recommended by other highly qualified professionals or organizations. How much should you bother? If your money is important to you, check!

- *Selective Disclosure*: Are your advisors letting sleeping dogs lie? Are your advisors only telling you what they want you to know so that you fulfill their agendas but not your own? The best defense against this problem is to get second opinions and work with a proactive team of high-level advisors.

- *Honesty*: You want advisors with integrity. If they can't answer a question, will they admit it and bring in specialists to help you? Many advisors won't call in specialists because they're afraid they'll lose you as a client if they seem less knowledgeable. Some are too greedy to let the revenue go to someone else, or their ego won't allow them to interact with other advisors. Look for advisors who are honest about their ability and capable of working with other advisors; together they will look out for your best interest.

- *If They Could Have, Why Didn't They?*: Never hesitate to ask yourself and your advisors this question: If your advisors could have helped you achieve your goals sooner, why didn't they? If your advisors knew about these options, why didn't they present them to you before?

- *Mathematical Analysis*: Seek advisors whose mathematical analysis makes sense. Ask questions centered around your personal goals and ask how a proposal, strategy or recommended action would mathematically affect your macro and micro needs. Make certain your advisors support their recommendations *for* or *against* a proposal with all of the facts and the math.

- *Get a Second Opinion*: Always get a second opinion on anything important, expensive, dangerous or painful. But beware of any advisor who uses the "Not Invented Here" stamp—who simply dismisses a proposal with, "Oh, that won't work for you." Ask, "Why not?," and keep asking until you are satisfied with the answers. Request an analysis demonstrating why the new proposal won't work for you.

- *Relationships*: Choose advisors who produce results and solutions, not those who use their relationships with you as the primary reason why you should do business with them. Don't let them tug on your heartstrings or push your fear buttons.

- *Don't be a Guinea Pig*: Important decisions or actions should always be addressed by the very best specialists available. Make sure your advisors are experts. Don't pay for a lot of research time. You don't want to be the test case for your advisor with the IRS. As a group, guinea pigs are not known for their high quality of life.

- *Think Global*: In many of life's important or complicated matters, we may have to look far and wide to obtain the necessary expertise to serve our interests. The world is full of people who are "conveniently located," but who lack the requisite skill and/or creativity to solve our problems. Convenience and success are often mutually exclusive concepts in the real world.

Only you can decide if you want the best. You decide the level of talent and cooperation on your team. One weak or egotistical player may cause you and your family to lose more than you can ever recover. Experts who perform at the highest level are available, if you look for them. Look for a talented, dedicated, honest, client-centered, creative team of specialists who will empower you to achieve your goals.

15

Thinking, Doing and Being the Elephant: How Elephants Choose Advisors

If you've gone through the goal-setting section of this book and you feel it makes sense to create a 100-year plan and develop a philosophy and an approach that are bigger than yourself, that involve your values and a higher purpose, then it makes sense that the advisors you select should be engaged in a similar thought process. In essence, if you've become a macro, see-the-elephant type of person, how is it going to profit you to deal with advisors who only deal with a little bit of the elephant and don't even acknowledge that the whole elephant exists? Many advisors don't even know what questions to ask to begin to see the elephant. Most advisors cannot comfortably engage in a conversation with you about a 100-year plan, about your philosophy, religious beliefs or goals. We must ask ourselves, "If our advisors don't know all of this important information about us, how can they make the best recommendations for us?"

Maybe a fair test of your advisors' perspective is to ask them how far into the future you should be thinking when you're doing your planning. If their response is, "You should look at a buy-and-hold strategy for at least a five-year period," then obviously you're dealing with people who are not macro-oriented. The answer I think we should be looking for is, "Well, what is your 100-year plan? What are your goals and philosophies of life? What are the values you hold dear, and what are you doing to further those values and achieve your highest and best purpose?" If they're not thinking in the 100-year frame, then what frame are they thinking in?

Over the years, clients who have consulted with me have recognized each other when they make references to "seeing the elephant." ("Hey! I'm working with a guy who tells the elephant story. . . . Do you know Bruce Wright, too?") The elephant, in fact, proved to be such a powerful image that it took on a life of its own. Pretty soon, clients who had assimilated the lesson and were ready to move on found that seeing the elephant wasn't enough; they started talking about *becoming* the elephant.

Once you learn to think macro and decide that "seeing the elephant" is a good perspective to have, you'll realize that it is a big improvement in vision. But, it isn't quite enough to just *see* the elephant; in essence, that's only the first step. Step two is acting on the improved vision. It's more rewarding and, naturally, that equates to "more difficult." Essentially, step two is this: Do and act like the elephant.

Adopting a 100-year planning approach is the beginning of this important step. Such thinking is "outside the box" and generally unknown amongst most professionals. Most people are consumed by their daily work, responsibilities, family and hobbies. Pushing thought and action outside of the normal process is far too rare.

How do you think? Earlier we discussed the differences between left-brain and right-brain thinking; the left side deals with the logical and the right side with the creative or emotional. Just as it was important for us to use both hemispheres of our brain in setting goals, it is also important to use both sides of our brain to think and do, so we can become an elephant. In so doing, we can achieve far greater breadth and depth of perception. Most of all, we'll get vastly superior results!

Far too often our advisors act like the blind men who argued over the nature of the elephant. Instead of realizing they needed each other, the six men acted like independent advisors who kill the other independent advisors' proposals. My experience has been that when all of the advisors work together to see the elephant, the client (or elephant) achieves the greatest level of satisfaction and performance. Each advisor should know what your answers are to the following questions and be working towards helping you achieve your goals. If you answer all of these questions to the best of your ability, you'll be able to clearly articulate your position for your advisors.

1. If you could wave a magic wand and create the perfect lifestyle or existence for your family, what would it be like? _____

_____

_____

_____

2. If you could throw away your calendar and replace it with one that took full advantage of your time, talent and resources, what would it look like? _____

_____

_____

_____

3. If you could change any list of things in the world, your community and your country, what would they be?

_____

_____

_____

4. How do you feel about your religion? _____

_____

_____

_____

5. How do you feel about your heirs? _____

_____

_____

_____

6. What would you like to provide for your heirs while you are alive? _____

_____

_____

_____

7. What would you like to provide for your heirs after your death? _____

_____

_____

_____

8. How do you feel about your spouse? _____

_____

_____

_____

9. What is preventing or delaying you from doing those things that are the best use of your time, talent and resources? _____

_____

_____

_____

10. Of your existing advisors, list those whose counsel you respect (friends, spouse, professionals, etc.). _____

_____

_____

_____

11. Of your existing advisors, who should be included in the decision-making process? _____

_____

_____

_____

12. What is the purpose of money? _____

_____

_____

The Trees are Falling

If a tree falls in the forest and nobody hears it, does it make a sound? This age-old question is directly relevant to your ability to achieve the perfect calendar. Let's look at it another way. If there is an opportunity in your life, but you don't act upon it, is it likely to benefit you? If there is a problem in your life, but you don't recognize it, misdiagnose it, or fail to take appropriate action, can it hurt you? If you don't _know_ you have cancer, can it kill you?

Right now while you are reading this, you probably have trees falling in your forest. The problem is that most of us are so distracted by life, we are relatively unaware of the danger around us. What's even worse is that perhaps your existing advisors don't recognize the trees that are about to fall either. The reason is pretty simple: Most advisors cannot answer the 12 questions about you that you just answered. Because they don't know and understand your feelings and preferences on these matters, they don't know what trees to look for.

Many professionals feel they do not need to be informed on "all that stuff." They rationalize most of it away by saying, "We don't do that here," or, "That's not my department," or, "That's someone else's responsibility." Most professionals and even companies that profess to be "full service" really do not know their clients. They lack the proactivity, training and skills to provide such high-level service. The newest trend with "full service" firms is the touting of "relationships." However, if you look closely enough, you'll find that it's usually just advertising fluff. (Although some of the ads *are* terrific!) The truth is, most advisors don't know what questions to ask their clients. Imagine what a difficult position most advisors would be in if a client actually gave them all of that data. What would they do with it? The traditional, independently acting advisor would want to create a proposal and submit it to the client. Of course, this almost never works with wealthy, sophisticated clients because they understand that no individual or company can advise them on everything and resolve all of their needs. As people become better informed and more sophisticated, they recognize the advantages of interdependence. They are unlikely to adopt proposals which do not incorporate input from their existing advisors or at least a team of highly competent specialists.

When you think about it, superior client understanding and service is the ultimate "sustainable competitive advantage." The A-level consumer's desire for truly value-enhanced service goes largely unmet because most professionals and their firms are too busy doing what they have always done. As people become more insistent upon the level of service I'm describing, what firms have always done becomes increasingly irrelevant. Professionals and companies who fail to meet the demands of a better informed market will lose their A-level clients to those who *know* and *do* deliver better client service.

16

Crocodiles With a Smile

If you are unaware of other people's agendas, it does you little good to have a firm grasp of your own. You must learn to recognize competing agendas to ensure that they don't interfere with yours.

I was introduced by telephone to Mr. B, a man who had recently been offered $14 million for his business. Mr. B was interested in accepting the offer, but wanted to be certain that the sale was structured in the most advantageous way for him and his family. At the conclusion of the telephone call, Mr. B asked if I would meet with John, the controller/treasurer of his corporation. He told me that John knew all of the details of his personal and business finances and was the "best guy to talk to about this sort of thing." Mr. B considered John a loyal advisor, friend and confidant.

Upon meeting with John, I discovered that John was not very enthusiastic about the opportunity at hand. John told me that Mrs. B had it in her mind that the business was worth $16 million and, since the offer was only for $14 million, Mrs. B would probably not go along with the sale. John touched on the fact that Mrs. B's father had started the business and there was some emotional element to the sale as well as the price issue. John and I agreed that it was a good idea to sell the business for all cash now; the couple were in their 70s and in declining health, so it was wise to use the current laws and opportunity to their best advantage while they were both mentally and physically able to do so. The tax laws and economy being what they were, a qualified buyer now was worth 20 in the bush. Once either of them died, many attractive options would disappear. Now was the time to act.

About a week later, I followed up with John regarding his progress toward sending me the financial data I had requested during our meeting. John informed me that it wouldn't be necessary to compile the data as Mrs. B had "killed the deal" because she felt the business was worth more. John reiterated that he felt the offer of $14 million cash was in fact very attractive. "Mrs. B just won't go for the sale. It's probably the emotional attachment as well as the price," John said.

I suggested to John that we review the numbers, then meet with Mr. and Mrs. B to present the information to them. After all, they should have a chance to see a macro left- and right-brain comparison of their current situation versus what their financial situation could be. Better knowledge usually makes for a better decision. The very important emotional issues could also be dealt with to Mrs. B's satisfaction.

At that point, John became agitated. "Look, this deal isn't going to happen," he told me. "That's all there is to it. Just drop the issue and don't call me or the B's again. If we need you, I'll call you."

Having encountered similar situations, I knew I wasn't getting the full story. I telephoned Mr. B's friend who had arranged the telephone introduction in the first place. I asked him if he knew what was going on. He said John had told the B's that he could perform the necessary analysis just fine on his own, and save them the cost of my fees. He had also told them that unless the offer was increased to at least the $16 million he thought the business was worth, there would be no need to do any analysis.

My fears were confirmed. John was not the loyal employee, friend and confidant the B's thought he was. His cooperative behavior was, at best, a facade.

What had happened? Why was John sabotaging the sale? In many situations it boils down to incongruent agendas. The B's were thinking: "Let's sell the company and cash in on all of our hard work and live happily ever after." John saw it differently: "I've worked my butt off to help this company. Why, if it wasn't for me, this company wouldn't be worth a dime. Now the B's are going to walk away rich and happy. What about me? I'm 61 years old and will be out of a job during a recession. It just isn't fair. Damn if I'll let this happen." Mr. and Mrs. B wanted what was best for their family. John wanted what was best for his. This is generally well and good, but when the game changes or is about to, things can fall apart in a hurry.

Even if John was not conscious of his feelings, they caused him to act in a way that was not in the best interest of the B's. John used Mrs. B's preconceived, overinflated value of the business as a "logical" reason not to make the deal. He had even planted this seed himself by saying to Mrs. B, "The business could be worth somewhere between $15 million and $16 million." Mrs. B's human tendency to latch onto the highest price took it from there. (Did you ever notice how most people list their homes with the real estate agent who tells them their homes are worth the most?)

Perhaps John even sabotaged the deal by preying on Mrs. B's emotions and saying something like, "Mrs. B, I know $14 million sounds like a good price, but it seems as if your father tried hard to keep this business in the family. Perhaps we should try to keep it in the family as well." Sometimes the "Johns" of the world don't want us to have real knowledge or information. They need us to be dependent on them. It is this dependence that gives them control and perceived value. They try to use our trust and vulnerabilities to manipulate us. Thus, they protect their position, money and power—and further their own agendas. If we are gullible enough and/or "John" is convincing enough, we never even know we've been sold out.

How can we avoid this type of situation in our own lives? We need to consider what other people's agendas might be. What do *they* want to accomplish? What is in *their* best interest? If Mr. and Mrs. B had asked themselves these questions about John, they might have found the answer to the situation. They might have realized that John was worried about how he could provide for himself and his family. He was worried about having a job. Once they came to this realization, John's advice could have been seen in a new light and the B's could have avoided being manipulated to meet John's agenda instead of their own. Perhaps a deal could have been structured, through the creativity of expert advisors, that would have met both the B's and John's agendas. The B's could have sold their business and retired as they had wanted to.

One key to becoming successful when making interdependent decisions is to understand the agendas of all the people involved and create win-win situations. So ask yourself, "What's in it for them?" It's also helpful to come right out and ask your advisors, "What's in it for you?" or "What are you hoping to get out of this?" Be wary of responses such as, "I'm just looking out for you." Sometimes it is helpful to have as guide an expert advisor who has been in these situations before. Such advisors can help you realize the potential dangers surrounding you, and they can be lifesavers.

I heard a story about a man who went on camera safari to a part of Africa where the leading cause of death was being eaten by crocodiles. The stories about the crocodiles were incredible. They could grow to be 18 feet long. They could outrun a world-class sprinter in a 20-yard dash. If a crocodile wanted you, a guide explained to the safari group the first night at the ranch, it was going to get you.

At dawn, guides woke the group up, bundled them into Land Rovers and drove off across the plains, all the while explaining the dangers of crocodiles. When they came to a river crossing, the travelers were told to stay inside the vehicles while each Land Rover was ferried across on a little barge, the guides warning everyone all the while not to get out. By this time, the man and his companions were starting to tune out the guides and say, "Okay, okay. We're not going to get near the crocodiles."

The Land Rovers set out again and entered a large grassy plain. Finally they came to a little hill rising above the plain and large enough for all the vehicles to park on. The people were grateful for the chance to get out of the vehicles and began looking through their binoculars for zebras, wildebeests and giraffes. After a while, the man noticed a large puddle at the base of the hill, about 50 yards away. The puddle looked to be about 10 feet in diameter and six or seven inches deep. He figured a lot of animals probably came to drink out of this puddle, so he took off down the hill, hoping maybe he'd see some lion tracks.

He was about halfway down the hill when one of the guides screamed at him, "Stop! Don't move!" His heart started pounding and he thought, "Oh my gosh! There must be a lion or something about to get me!" The guide continued, "Very slowly, very carefully walk backwards, back up the hill, the same way you came down." Now the guy was scared to death. Just as he was thinking about turning and running toward the top of the hill, the guide yelled, "Move slowly. No sudden movements." So the man backed slowly up the hill away from the puddle, his heart racing and his adrenaline pumping with every step. When he got to the top, he was still scared, but now he was embarrassed, too, because all 20 people in the group had turned and were watching him.

"I just saved you from the crocodiles," the guide said.

Now the man became angry because he felt he'd been frightened and embarrassed without just cause. So he said to the guide, "I don't appreciate you making a spectacle out of me in front of all these people. There are obviously no crocodiles in that little mud puddle down there!"

The guide shook his head and said, "Obviously you're not familiar with the terrain here. What you don't know is that three or four weeks ago this mound we're on was an island. As far as you can see was under water. But now the rainy season has ended, and the dry season has begun. The water has evaporated or seeped down into underground rivers. You see this dry plain, but there are scattered puddles throughout the area, and crocodiles congregate in those puddles. They wallow around in there and dig them out to make them a little bit deeper, and they hide themselves so that the only thing sticking out of the water is their nostrils, ears, and eyeballs. Until you're right up on them, you can't see them. They wait, and as soon as an animal comes down to get a drink of water, the crocodiles jump out of the water and grab it. As we told you before, crocodiles can outrun human beings in the mud. You really don't stand a chance."

The man, still on edge and feeling even more stupid now, said, "That sounds like a great story, except I'm not falling for it."

The guide responded, "Why don't you pick up a rock and throw it into the puddle?"

The man picked up a rock and hurled it into the water. Two crocodiles, both more than 10 feet in length, came snapping out of the puddle. Finally the man realized that he could have been their lunch.

Why is this story relevant? Remember Mr. and Mrs. B? John, the controller, was a crocodile. Mr. and Mrs. B were not familiar with the terrain, and they didn't know the nature of the game that was being played. They were tourists in the advanced wealth management arena. It didn't matter how much skill or experience they had in other areas. They couldn't recognize that their "friend and advisor" was not only a crocodile, but that he was the worst kind of crocodile—a crocodile with a smile.

17

Billy Bob, the One-Stop Shop

No one professional advisor can keep abreast of the rapidly growing body of information regarding advanced wealth management. The information age is fully upon us and progressing at lightning speed. Newspapers, special reports, newsletters, magazines, seminars, e-mail, the Internet—all of these means of communication provide more information than one person can assimilate. The day of the specialist is here. The one-stop-financial-shop no longer works. Specialists, not generalists, are needed to handle the breadth and depth of our financial needs. No one person can expertly handle all aspects of these complicated issues.

Suppose you took your pet fish to a veterinarian and while you were there, you mentioned that you had a headache. "How long have you had it?" asks the vet.

You begin to answer, "I've had the headache for a couple of weeks, but I've been afraid to go to the doctor because . . ." when the vet interrupts you.

"Would you like me to check it out?" she asks.

Hesitantly, you reply, "Sure."

The veterinarian shines a light in your eyes, pokes and prods you for awhile, and says, "Well, it looks as if a small tumor is developing. But don't worry, I can fix you right up. A little laser incision just above the temple, and we'll have that puppy right out of there."

You're flabbergasted and ask, "Have you ever done anything like this before?"

She says, "Oh, yeah. I've done one pig, two iguanas and a goat so far this year. But don't worry, I've read a couple of articles on how it's done with people."

By the shocked look on your face, the vet can tell you're not convinced that she is the right person for the job. So the vet adds, "I'll cut you a deal. I'll do it on an outpatient basis in one afternoon and have you home in time for supper. Best of all, I'll only charge you a fraction of what a real specialist like a brain surgeon would charge you."

Now, I know these circumstances seem ridiculous, but when you think about it, this type of situation occurs all the time—albeit in a less obvious fashion. A couple goes to see their stock broker to sell some stock and they mention the need for some estate planning. "Don't worry," says the stock broker, "I can do that for you." Or a client meets with a corporate attorney and happens to mention the need for some advanced strategic planning. "Don't worry," the corporate attorney says, "I can do that for you."

In the medical profession, there are far more checks and balances in place than in the financial services industry. You won't find a general practitioner in the medical profession who does brain surgery on the side. If you ask a cardiologist about a problem you're having with regard to your brain wave pattern, the cardiologist is not going to prescribe treatment. However, there are attorneys who will give you all kinds of suggestions about investments even though they're not registered investment advisors. Your insurance agent may pick up your living trust legal document, review it for you for free and tell you what's good, bad or indifferent about it. Clearly that agent is not in a position to legally render such an opinion. But it happens anyway.

The financial services industry needs more discipline. Financial professionals should realize they act best as specialists and work together as a team. It is in the best interest of the client and the professional to refer clients to other specialists who can help them. The clients would get better service and advice, and the advisors wouldn't waste their time trying to figure out something that is outside their area of expertise. In this day of specialization, the financial industry needs to take its cue from the medical profession.

Why wouldn't an advisor refer a client to someone who is a level 9 or 10 specialist in the area of the client's needs? Here are three answers to that question:

1. *Fear* — Some advisors feel that if they refer you, they will appear less knowledgeable. They fear you might be inclined to hire someone who seems to have greater knowledge, skill, creativity, perspective or talent. They fear losing you as a client.

2. *Greed* — If you turn to someone else for advice, the new advisor will receive the revenue instead of the existing advisor.

3. *Ego* — Nearly every productive person has some degree of ego. At some level, you might call this confidence. But some advisors' egos won't allow them to acknowledge that they don't know everything. And some advisors' egos prohibit them from working with other advisors.

If you were on trial for murder, would you want a divorce attorney defending you? Would you rather have an expert macro strategic planner help you structure your wealth, or a life insurance salesperson? Each specialist has his or her place and an important function to perform, but one person shouldn't think he or she can be the one all-knowing advisor. And as a client, you should know that one person cannot be your one-stop-shop financial advisor. You need a team of expert advisors. When something as important as your personal or family wealth is involved, get the best help available. Would you rather have a veterinarian or a neurosurgeon performing your brain surgery?

18

Egomaniacs on the Loose

Not only will egomaniac advisors discourage you from seeking expert advice, some advisors' egos will even prevent them from being able to work with the advisors you have in place. This trait is especially detrimental in advanced wealth management because such activities require a team of expert specialist advisors to effectively plan strategies and implement tactics to enable you to achieve your goals. Beware of advisors who are too big for their britches: they can be the weak links in your chain of advisors.

Highly competent advisors will feel comfortable with the team approach. They put the client's best interests ahead of their own egos and agendas. The best results are produced when all the advisors participate in the process. When working with my personal clients, I always *try* to bring existing advisors into the loop. I include them in the process to help them understand what the client's goals, thoughts and feelings really are. Then, collectively, we work to develop a consensus about the options available to help the client achieve his or her goals and objectives. The attorney, accountant, stock broker, real estate agent, life insurance agent, banker, all the different players who are involved in the client's decision in any way are part of the team making the recommendations. Unfortunately, sometimes we come across advisors who cannot put their own egos or agendas aside and do what's best for the client.

I was working with a client whose attorney would not send us copies of the client's existing will and trust documents for us to review. The attorney said his reason for not cooperating with this request was that if he were to send us legal documents and we were to review them, we'd be "practicing law without a license." That was his excuse. When we discussed the situation with the client, the reaction was one of surprise. The client had checked our references and knew that we had a long-standing record of success and good references from leading law firms. The client decided to work with a more cooperative law firm.

(Changing lawyers turned out to be an extremely good decision. Two years later, the uncooperative attorney was indicted on charges of fraud. He had made himself the trustee of a number of estates and had in essence stolen many millions of dollars and fled the country. Eventually he was apprehended and sent to prison. Unfortunately, his clients never got their money back.)

What should you think when attorneys, accountants, stock brokers or any advisors don't want to share information or let anyone else review their work? What should you think when advisors feel they should be the only ones making recommendations? You should ask yourself, "What are they trying to hide? Why won't they cooperate with anybody?" Is it because there's something wrong with their work? Are they ripping you off? Or is their ego so out of control that they think they're the only person who has any answers?

Whether they are doing something wrong or their egos are simply too huge, either reason is cause for alarm and caution. Truly excellent advisors are proactive and open-minded.

Really good advisors welcome the opportunity for others to review their work. It's an opportunity to showcase their work and an opportunity to expand their referral network. If you do good work, you want other people to see it. It may lead to more business. If you show your work to another advisor and it's good, there's a strong chance that the person will say, "You know, you really did a good job on this. I've got a couple of clients who could use some help like this. Would you be interested in working on their situations?" Any competent professional would welcome a chance to network and work with other advisors.

There is one more common problem an advisor's ego can cause clients. Sometimes a large ego produces an advisor who's "a talker, not a doer."

Our clients Mark and Joanne had attended a whole bunch of seminars and talked to a lot of people in their search for the perfect plan before deciding on our services. At one point, they had constructed a plan they thought was pretty good, but then they learned about charitable trusts and family limited partnerships. So they resumed their search for information with a new round of seminars and advice-gathering. Unfortunately they wasted much of their time receiving advice that was not objective because they talked to many salespeople masquerading as consultants. These people really had a product to sell. Finally, they hired an attorney whom they had heard lecture and asked him to set up their family limited partnership.

This attorney billed himself as the local "guru" of family partnerships and charitable trusts. Six months after they hired him, the attorney still had done nothing. They wrote him a couple of letters expressing their desire to move ahead with their planning, to which he didn't respond. Mark and Joanne learned the hard way that this man's ego fed on lecturing. He was a talker, not a doer. Although many expert advisors are also adept lecturers and speakers, this attorney was an egomaniac who didn't seem to do anything except lecture and write articles. They needed to find someone who performed and produced results.

So beware of the egomaniac who won't refer clients, who won't work with other advisors and who doesn't produce results. There are few things more frustrating than discovering too late that an advisor's ego has not only cost you hundreds of thousands of dollars in fees and lost opportunities, but also cost you in happiness or peace of mind.

19

The Good Ol' Boys and Girls

One of the problems we face when selecting advisors is the "Good Ol' Boys and Girls" network. "The Good Ol' Boys and Girls" can be a circle of advisors who are established in a certain geographic area, or it can even be just one particular advisor in an area. The identifying feature of advisors involved in this kind of network is the common goal to block outside opinion or competition. The people who fall into this category do not want their clients to receive any advice, input or thoughts, let alone actual recommendations, from anyone other than themselves. In their attempts to keep other information out, members of this group can resort to deceit, lying and other unethical behavior. If by some chance their clients do encounter other information, the advisors participating in the "Good Ol' Boys and Girls" mentality will immediately reject it.

This problem is particularly apparent in many small communities because the network is smaller, tighter and placed under a microscope. There isn't as much competition, and usually the members of the network are well established in the area. This does not mean there are no good advisors in small communities. But you should be cautioned against the advisor or circle of advisors who block outside opinion or immediately reject outside recommendations. Many ideas and concepts that could benefit these advisors' clients are never even discussed with them. Sometimes advanced concepts and strategies that could help the client fall outside of these advisors' paradigms, so the advisors simply dismiss them.

These advisors usually have little desire to expand their knowledge because they have become complacent. Perhaps they are too lazy to continue learning by traveling outside their immediate location or revenue focus. They are "campers" rather than "climbers." They usually cannot rate at level 7 or higher in the "Rate Your Knowledge" exercise in a larger community. They will *never* rate 9 or 10.

In their defense, part of the result of being in a small community is that these advisors tend to extend themselves to service a broader need in the community. They become the general practitioner. In a small community, they can't make a living if they are too specialized because the demand for specialized services is not there.

However, it is more a matter of mental geography than of actual physical location. For example, both California towns of Camarillo and Westlake Village have a population of approximately 100,000 people. Yet an attorney in Camarillo has restricted himself to local business and considers his market to be Camarillo and nearby Ventura. Another attorney in Westlake Village considers the state of California to be his market. There is tremendous disparity between the work done by these two lawyers. The lawyer in Westlake has far more vision and experience than the attorney in Camarillo.

Why? By restricting his focus to just Camarillo and Ventura, the Camarillo lawyer sees far fewer situations than the Westlake attorney. Because he sees fewer situations, the Camarillo lawyer gets less experience. The more cases an attorney looks at and works on, the more experience he or she gains. The added experience is very important to you as a client. You can be unjustly restricted by an advisor's limited perspective. If you're having brain surgery, you want the surgeon to have successfully completed many such operations; you don't want to be the guinea pig. With matters such as brain surgery and your macro strategic planning, you want to have advisors who are skilled and who have successfully cured many patients or have successfully structured many comprehensive plans. Don't be the test case for your advisor with the IRS. When something as important as your financial future is at stake, get the best help available. Remember, sometimes you may need to go outside your local geographic area for sufficient expertise. At least remember to get a second opinion.

If you do mention or show something to your advisor, and he or she dismisses it with, "Oh, that won't work for you," ask "Why not?" Often, the advisor responding in that way is not familiar with the information or strategy presented, and the response is an attempt to avoid admitting ignorance. Something that appears difficult, complicated or costly to learn, implement or make available to clients will often be summarily dismissed.

We've discussed how fear, ego and greed can cloud an advisor's response and put his or her agenda ahead of yours. And fear, ego, and greed can be amplified if they are compounded with incompetence or ignorance. Don't let your advisors block outside information by simply dismissing it. Whenever an advisor makes a recommendation either for or against a proposal, always ask "Why?" And it's always appropriate to ask for a written analysis that supports the conclusions. Nobody cares about your financial success as much as *you* do. So, it's up to *you* to make sure you're getting the best advice possible.

20

Let Sleeping Dogs Lie

'**L**et sleeping dogs lie." This is a phrase I will never forget, and I hope you'll remember it, too, when it comes to selecting advisors.

I was sitting in a real estate agent's office getting ready for a meeting with her client, Ted. He was considering putting an industrial building he owned into a tax-exempt trust. We were going over the facts of the case when Jean, the real estate agent, said, "We need to get this done in about 45 minutes because an apartment building Ted's selling is falling out of escrow today. We want to try to put it back into escrow, so we're going to renegotiate with the buyers and make some changes in the deal."

That information about the apartment building changed Ted's "big picture" situation. Ted wanted to reduce his stress and increase his income by selling some of his real estate holdings. Once Ted put a piece of property into a tax-exempt trust, he could sell it free of capital gains tax. The proceeds could then be invested to produce income for Ted. However, there cannot be a "pre-arranged sale" on an asset going into a tax-exempt trust. Because the apartment building was in escrow, it could not have gone into a tax-exempt trust because it would have been considered a "pre-arranged sale." But now that the apartment building was falling out of escrow and the deal was going to have to be renegotiated, it could be put into a tax-exempt trust before it entered escrow again.

So I said to the real estate agent, "If that property is falling out of escrow and you've got a buyer ready to move ahead, why don't we put the apartment building into the tax-exempt trust as opposed to the industrial building we've been considering? Later, we can decide what percentage, if any, of that industrial building should go into the trust. This would be better for Ted because he could use the tax deduction created by putting the apartment building into the tax-exempt trust to offset some or all of the taxes on the sale of the industrial building."

She replied, "Look, I've worked a really long time in order to get this thing put together, and I don't want to lose this buyer. I don't want to waste the time it would take to get this trust created."

I told her it would only take 72 hours to put the transaction together and get the documentation, but she insisted, "No, no, no, we could lose the buyer."

Jean had been telling the client and me that it was a pretty strong market and that she wouldn't have any problem getting buyers. When I questioned her on that issue, she became noticeably upset.

"This is my client. This is my case. I'm bringing you in, and I don't want you to even discuss this apartment building with the client, because you should just let sleeping dogs lie," she said.

I explained that I couldn't do that. My responsibility is to represent the best interest of the client. It was in Ted's best interest to look at the big picture, not just to focus on the industrial building going into the tax-exempt trust as a single, isolated transaction. He needed to know about this new development with the apartment building and the new options available.

At what expense was I suppose to let sleeping dogs lie? In this case, at the expense of $300,000 in unnecessary taxes that Ted would have to pay. Why did Jean want me not to disclose all the information to Ted? So Jean could make $75,000 in commissions. She could still have her $75,000 in commissions, just three days later. And, if she did have to find a new buyer, maybe it would be an extra month or two before she received her commission. But should the client be willing to lose $300,000 in order for her to make $75,000 on this transaction a few days or weeks sooner? This is an obvious conflict of interest. Any honest, competent person will see the ethical problem.

So what happened? The real estate agent admitted that she wanted to work with me on the case and she trusted me by reputation to do this properly. She realized it would not be fair to the client not to disclose all of the options. So Ted came in and we talked about the situation.

He said, "You know, it makes sense to look at the whole picture instead of just looking at the industrial building. Maybe we should step back and look at this apartment building falling out of escrow as an opportunity to either renegotiate with the existing buyer or get another buyer."

As I was driving back from the meeting, I received an agitated call from Jean on my cellular phone. After I had left, she and Ted had met with the buyers and explained the change in direction they wanted to take. The buyers did not appreciate the change and gave her and Ted a hard time by saying, "Once you get that set up, let us know and maybe we'll consider the building again. But we're not going to sit here and negotiate with you if you're not in a position to do so. It's a waste of everybody's time."

Jean was furious. She was afraid she was going to have to find a new buyer for the property. As I listened to her complain about the results of not letting sleeping dogs lie, I thought, "We can help the client through combined planning and tactics save approximately $750,000 in taxes. He could put that money to work for him for the rest of his life, which would dramatically increase his net spendable income, give him some tax deductions, free up some of his money, give him some liquidity, diversification, all the things he wants. And she's upset because she might have lost this buyer, and she might have to wait to get her commission."

As the deal developed over the next couple of days, Ted told me he had decided that his real estate agent's only job was to find buyers for his property. He was retaining my firm to represent his best interest. He wanted us in the deal because we were apparently the only company he had in the loop that was objectively, competently and creatively looking out for his best interest.

In this case, Ted had taken a look at his advisor's agenda and seen that she was in it for the commission. He was able to retain her services—she was great at finding buyers—but he had taken control of his situation and was looking out for his own agenda.

How can you tell whether or not the people you've selected are providing you with all the expertise you need? Are you really getting the best advice possible? Are your existing advisors doing a thorough job, or are they letting sleeping dogs lie? Are you exposed to *all* the options? An advisor may have a different agenda from yours. In some cases, advisors will only tell you what *you* would like to hear. I guess you could call them "yes-men." Some advisors will only tell you what *they* would like you to hear. Sometimes they'll tell you just enough to entice you to do what they want you to do. They have accomplished their purpose, and you only think you have achieved your goal. Stay away from advisors who want to just let sleeping dogs lie, who don't want to explore all the options or disclose all of the information.

The best defense against this type of selective disclosure is to get a second opinion and to work with a team of advisors.

Let's talk about the value of a second opinion for a minute. If one doctor suggested to you that you needed to have brain surgery, and you were a thinking person, you would want to get a second or even a third opinion. Why don't people exercise the same level of discretion in their financial decision-making? Why wouldn't you get a second or third opinion? It amazes me that people will engage in multimillion dollar transactions without doing even remotely close to the same amount of homework, research and discovery as they would if they were going on vacation.

You have to discipline yourself to get a second opinion. That's where the responsibility begins and ends—with you.

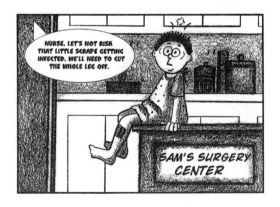

Always get a second opinion on anything painful, expensive or important.

21

Why Didn't You Tell Me About This When . . .

A very large, well respected law firm asked me to engage in seminars with them to educate their clients on macro strategic planning and some of the tactics discussed in this book. I agreed to speak, and so the particular partner I was dealing with went back to his other partners to talk about the seminars, get budget approval and so forth. The partners turned him down.

He called me up and said, "I'm really embarrassed by this, but they don't want to do the seminars because of the liability problem."

I was younger and more naive back then. I said, "I don't get it. Liability problem? You're a law firm. Your job is to look out for liability problems."

He replied, "Yeah, I know, but I don't think you really understand the kind of liability we're talking about here. You see," he said, "we're afraid a lot of our clients who should have heard about these ideas before are going to be upset because they didn't hear about them. Perhaps they engaged in strategies or tactics that were not as effective. Even if they would not have utilized the information we would be presenting in the seminar, the law firm had an obligation to disclose to them all of the options. If we failed to show them these options, then we were negligent. If clients make the claim that they might have implemented certain strategies or tactics had they known about them, and the strategies would have saved them *x* amount of dollars in taxes, we have a liability problem. We become liable for that because we charged them fees for advice and then we didn't represent them to the extent they were entitled to be represented."

Now this is one of the most honest attorneys I've dealt with. He was being straight with me. Of course the partners would have had an absolute fit had they known he had disclosed their deep, dark secret to me. But I would submit to you that there are a tremendous number of law firms with that type of liability problem today—as well as banks, accounting firms and financial services firms. They should tell their clients about macro strategic planning and various wealth management tactics, but they may be afraid to do so because of their past failure to disclose pertinent options.

What happens when a client says, "This sounds great. If it's been around for awhile, why didn't you tell me about it before?"

I was sitting in a meeting where that exact question was raised. After presenting some strategies and tactical options to a client, the client looked at his attorney and accountant and said, "Why didn't you tell me about this before? If you had told me about this before I sold my building last year, I would have saved $1 million in capital gains taxes and I would have saved another $115,000 in income taxes. How come you're just telling me about this now?"

The advisors furtively looked at each other and the accountant said, "Well, this is not my area of expertise," and passed the plate to the attorney.

The attorney, realizing the real estate agent involved in that deal was not present to defend himself, said, "That was a real estate transaction, so that was the real estate agent's responsibility."

Fortunately, the client was smart enough to know that wasn't really the case. But he liked this attorney and accountant, and they were trying to do something about it, so he didn't sue them and didn't file any complaints.

And I must say, you have to give some credit to that attorney and accountant, because at least they were trying to rectify the situation and present other available options, whereas I think the majority of professionals in this country when faced with a situation like that would not even bring it to the client's attention.

What if somebody else brings the situation to the client's attention, some outsider, what do you think that attorney and accountant are going to do?

They're going to call each other up on the phone and say, "We've got a problem here. If our clients implement the tactics this outside person is recommending, they're going to realize that they should have done this on some of their past transactions. We're going to be cooked! Our liability coverage is going to go through the roof, and we're going to lose our clients. We've got to defeat this thing right here and now."

So they develop a little pact that works something like this: Their client, Joe, has been doing business with them for a while. When Joe brings in a proposal from an outside consultant, the accountant may chuckle and say, "You know, Joe, I've been your accountant for 15 years and I've seen a lot of cockamamie, half-baked ideas before, but I think this one tops them all. Let me see if I've got this right: Your stock broker and a so-called consultant gave you these ideas and strategies? Well, all I can say is that if stock brokers and consultants were qualified, don't you think they'd have 'CPA' after their names?"

The attorney may use a similar tactic with Joe by saying, "As you know, I've got a master's degree in taxation. You can trust me when I tell you this just doesn't make any sense for you at all. Did they explain the negatives to you? Do you know some of these strategies are irrevocable? You can never change your mind. Did they really emphasize that? Let me tell you a couple of horror stories of things I've seen."

Joe listens to these buffoons and doesn't do what he could have, should have, would have done. Why? Because he didn't do several of the things we've talked about.

- He didn't ask himself, "What's in it for them?" He didn't recognize their agendas and check to see if they were in alignment with his.

- He let them dismiss the recommendations by saying, "Oh, this won't work for you." He didn't ask them, "Why not?" and ask them to support their opinions with *written* analysis.

- He didn't ask to see their recommendations of alternatives and the mathematical analysis that supported their positions.

- He fell for the "Get in, sit down and shut up" tactic that both the CPA and the attorney were using by flashing their designations at him.

- He didn't ask them the question, "Why didn't you tell me about this when . . . ?"

There's another mistake Joe made. He let his advisors tug on his heartstrings, he let them tie him down by using their relationships with him to their advantage. It's easier to do nothing than to take action. It's easier to trust these people who have been doing you a disservice by not providing all of the options to you for the last 15 years than it is to take action with people who are new and unfamiliar to you. Joe didn't know where to look for crocodiles.

22

If They Could Have, Why Didn't They?

I was referred to a potential client, Bob, who realized the importance of asking the question, "If they could have, why didn't they?" Bob wanted to retire, relax, travel and benefit several charitable organizations in his area. He had been working with an attorney and accountant for 15 years who had been unable to help him reach those goals even though he was worth approximately $20 million. A colleague and I constructed a plan which would enable Bob to restructure his net worth in such a way that he would be able to accomplish his goals.

During the course of an unrelated conversation with his existing lawyer, Bob mentioned the plan that I was working on for him. The attorney's ears pricked up, and he asked Bob to send him and the accountant a copy of the plan so that they could review it. The attorney and accountant were good friends and had a long-standing relationship with each other and with Bob. Quite frankly, they were very discouraged and upset that Bob was talking to outside people. They were concerned they might, in fact, lose their client, who was a substantial client in terms of the legal and accounting fees paid to them annually by Bob's businesses.

After the attorney and accountant reviewed our recommendations, they told Bob the recommendations sounded attractive, but they had some very deep concerns about their workability. They felt Bob should not take any action until he really considered all of the options available to him.

Those advisors were right. Bob needed to consider all of the options before he implemented anything. But Bob also needed to insist that these advisors, who had known him so well for so long, present him with other recommendations and options.

It's very simple for advisors to say, "Well, I just don't think this will work for you. I've known you for a long time, and I just don't think these strategies or tactics will work for you. I think you should be worried about this, this and this." They hit all of the emotional buttons and scare the bejeepers out of the client. They use their relationships with the client to their fullest advantage. The client ends up doing nothing and suffering in the same situation he or she was trying to get out of.

I suggested to the client that he ask the attorney and accountant what other options existed that were not being considered. The attorney and accountant could not answer that question. They could not help Bob achieve his goals. If they could have, why didn't they? Why, for 15 years, had they not resolved his situation? Because they couldn't. If your advisors shoot down proposals from other advisors, ask them, "Why? What's wrong with this proposal? What better proposal can you offer?" And remember, if they could have fixed your situation beforehand, why didn't they?

It is not uncommon for existing advisors to play on the emotions and attack all of the client's fear points by saying, "This is going to be complicated. It's going to be frightening. What if it doesn't work out? What are you going to do later? What if they mess it up? Who are these people? You've never dealt with them." (All valid questions, I'll agree.) They say, "You can trust me. I'll take care of you as I always have." Often the practical reality is that these people have never adequately taken care of the client. If they had, the client would not be coming to us.

There are situations even worse than laziness and complacency. I've seen advisors who, having thought the situation out, decided it was better for them *not* to solve the client's problem. Let's take a look at that for just a minute.

Without a properly constructed strategic plan, there would have been problems when either Bob or his wife passed away because they had each brought separate assets to their marriage. There were opportunities for some very hefty legal and accounting fees, to the tune of hundreds of thousands of dollars, to "sort through" everything and "fix" everything. "Don't worry," the advisors might tell the surviving spouse, "We'll get to the bottom of this. We'll fix this for you."

Hundreds of thousands of dollars later, yes, it would be fixed. It would be resolved in some way, but would it really be resolved in the optimum way for the client? I would say that in most cases it would not be nearly as good for either the clients or their heirs as it could have been had these things been put in order before one or both of the spouses passed away.

Let's take a look at it from the accountant's position. The accountant thinks to himself, "Gee, if Bob sells this business so he can retire, there goes a $50,000-a-year account. I'm 60 years old. I'm getting ready to retire in a couple of years myself. I'm thinking about selling my interest in this accounting partnership to my partners. I need as many clients as I can possibly get and maintain so that the value of my interest in the business is increased." If it's a sole practitioner selling his practice, then it's even more obvious. The more clients there are, the more income is generated annually, the greater the selling price of the accounting business. And the accountant thinks, "Boy, if Bob sells this business, I won't be working on this case any more because it's almost guaranteed that whoever buys Bob's business is going to bring in their own people to handle the accounting issues. So, if I go along with this deal, this is going to be a problem for me. I just think he ought to do something else."

The logical questions the client ought to be asking the existing advisors are, "What else should I be doing? You say I should explore the other options. Well, what are they? I've got all this evidence telling me these outside advisors have put together an effective way to solve my problems. They say that they've looked at all of the options."

Bob's existing advisors didn't even know what all of the options were. They didn't know what the remaining options were over and above what we had written down in the recommendations. If they did know, then they should have sat the client down and explained all of the options, put them all in writing and provided the numbers. So we're back to that nagging question once again, "If they could have, why didn't they?" Ask yourself this question about your existing advisors. Why aren't you fulfilled? Why aren't you where you want to be? Why are you reading this book?

Did you have to go buy this book, or did you have the good fortune to meet an advisor who wants to help you see the big picture and who gave you this book in an effort to help you break through the barriers that may be holding you back?

If you haven't heard of these issues before or discussed them with your advisors, don't let those advisors fool you. Some advisors are incapable of representing you on these issues. If they were capable, they would have already done so. Instead they're going to cost you money and time. If they won't cooperate or don't know how to do this work, it's going to take longer to implement the strategies that will achieve your goals. The longer it takes, the more billable hours are involved. And if you decide that the relationship with that advisor is more important than achieving your goals, then that advisor is likely to cost you more than you can ever recover.

Maybe you're going to have to lose an advisor. Maybe you can just set the advisor aside temporarily and use specialists to handle a particular issue. If you're going in for brain surgery, you're not going to have the general practitioner do it. You want a specialist, a neurosurgeon. If that hurts the general practitioner's ego, too bad. Don't reward advisors who have ego problems and competency problems by insisting that they be involved. Get good-quality, competent people around you and use them. If your existing people can fit into that category, can work well in that type of system, even learn from it, then great. Maybe they can become more competent and effective. If they're incapable of making the adjustment, then leave them behind. Move on to the next level. This is your money. It's your future. It's your life and legacy.

23

Not Invented Here

There's a rubber stamp you never get to see, but which definitely exists. It's the "Not Invented Here" stamp, and far too many advisors have one and use it often. It's the mental label they slap on any recommendations they didn't make themselves.

One thing you can count on when people are making a proposal to you is that 99.9% of the time they're going to say, "I've looked at everything, and I think this is the best thing for you to do." For example, an insurance representative comes out and shows you a particular insurance policy. It has certain features and certain costs associated with it. You look at it and ask, "Is that the best thing for me?" The advisor replies, "I really believe it's the best thing for you." Isn't that what every professional is going to tell you?

So you say, "Thank you very much. I'm going to give it some thought." You take the insurance proposal to another insurance professional or other advisor for a second opinion. What do they do? They come up with something they say is better. It almost never fails. In fact, it might even be the same policy with the same company and all they've done is change the terms somewhat.

For example, the first proposal may have been a very honest representation of the facts and figures and assumed a conservative interest rate of 6%. The second person who is reviewing the proposal is almost always automatically going to stamp it "Not Invented Here" or "Doesn't Put Money in My Pocket."

The second advisor will then come up with a counter proposal: perhaps the very same policy with the same company, but with an assumed interest rate one percent higher. The uninformed, unwary consumer believes the second proposal is better. The problem is that the consumer could find three, four, five or six additional proposals that are going to appear to be better. If you don't know that's the way the game is played, you might choose the second proposal because you think it's a better deal, not knowing that if you had purchased the policy from the first guy, you would have gotten exactly the same product and exactly the same real rate of return. The only difference was an illusion played with the interest rate assumption and the computer analysis. That's all. One guy was being more conservative and perhaps more honest than the other guy.

The "Not Invented Here" stamp is not unique to the insurance business. Let's assume you have a piece of real estate that is giving you management headaches, and you want to get rid of it. A real estate agent says, "Here's what you ought to do. You ought to do a 1031 exchange. You ought to take this property and exchange it for this other property. This is what it's going to cost and these are going to be the benefits." A second person comes in and says, "No, you ought to put the property in a tax-exempt trust and sell it within the trust. These are the costs, and these are the benefits. Here are the advantages and disadvantages." You like the second proposal better, but out of loyalty to the first person, you call him or her and say, "I've got this other proposal, and it's even better." The first person, not wanting to lose you as a client says, "I can do that too. If you want to go that way, I can do that. And you should implement it with me because . . . ." and the tug of war begins with you in the middle. Each side trying to get a better foothold and grasp on you by tweaking the proposal just a bit.

I remember the first life insurance policy I bought. The insurance agent, George, was married to an old girlfriend of mine. He called me up and introduced himself. I had no idea who he was until he told me, "I'm Joyce's husband." "Oh, yeah, sure. Joyce is a friend of mine," I said. Then he got to the point of his call, "I'm with this insurance company, and we need to get together." I agreed out of some feeling of allegiance to Joyce.

He came to our apartment and sat down with my wife and me. At one point during the process of trying to sell us life insurance, he looked at me and asked, "Bruce, do you love your wife?" How could I answer in any way but in the affirmative? She was sitting there right next to me, and I do, in fact, love my wife.

"Well, yes I do," I answered.

He said, "You know, you really need to buy this insurance because if you love your wife, you wouldn't want to leave her in this terrible position."

He proposed buying a $50,000 whole life policy on my life with a $25,000 rider if my wife died. The way he put it was, "At this stage of your life, if you love somebody, chances are if you lose that person, you're not going to be able to work. You're not going to be able to function. You're going to need to be financially capable of taking six months off until you can start to get past the grief."

When it came down to the price issue, we wavered, and he made his final point: "You know, Bruce, life insurance is like a parachute. You only need it once, but you never know when you're going to need it."

That was the way he left us, because we weren't going to give him a check right then. We wanted to talk about it between ourselves. That night I had dreams about falling out of an airplane and not having a parachute and thinking, "My gosh, this is a responsibility I have for the one I love." We bought the insurance from him.

Later on, when we were about to have our first child, I talked to another insurance agent, Ron, who convinced me that instead of keeping the $50,000 coverage on my life and $25,000 on my wife, we should convert to a term insurance policy. We could change companies, and for the same amount of money we were paying for the amount of coverage we had with the first company through George, we could have $500,000 of life insurance on myself and $250,000 on my wife. Ron argued that the savings features of the whole life insurance policy paled by comparison to the cash we would need if death really occurred.

If my wife died, how much money would I need to hire somebody to come in and look after our child while I went to work? How much money would I need to be able to pay for the funeral and associated expenses? When your loved one dies, you don't want to go into debt and have to make funeral payments every month for the next five years. It's hard to put the grief behind you when you're writing a check out for the funeral expenses every month. The $25,000 we had on my wife was not enough.

If I died, $500,000 was the absolute minimum necessary for my wife to replace my income. If she took the $500,000 and invested it to produce income at the then prevailing interest rates, or at a conservative estimate of what interest rates might be in the future, she would be able to live off the income and not work. This was important to us because we had made a decision that my wife would raise our children and not work simultaneously. I thought Ron's arguments made a lot of sense. So I canceled the first policy and went with Ron's company.

Well, when George got the notice from his insurance company saying that we had canceled the policy, it obviously affected his renewal commission. I also learned that George had made roughly three times more commission by selling us the whole life policies than if he had sold us the term policies—even though we would have received 10 times the amount of coverage. It seemed to me that Ron was being more responsible in looking out for the needs of my family and me, whereas George was either A.) technically incompetent or incapable of really helping us, or B.) looking out for his own interest. So whether he was being dishonest or whether he was incompetent really didn't matter. I didn't want to work with him in either case.

Well, George called and was very nice and personable about things. I agreed to let him come over because he was, after all, Joyce's husband. He came over to the house and we started talking about the situation. I explained the arguments that Ron had made. George agreed with Ron's reasoning. He said, "Now that you have a child, I think I agree with Ron. Remember when I first sold you this policy, I said over time your needs would change and we'd need to get together and revisit this issue. Ron's philosophy is absolutely right, but I've known you a long time. Joyce and I appreciate your business. I can implement those same recommendations for you through my company." I told George I would think about it.

And I did think about it. I've thought about it a lot over the years. I've encountered similar situations with the same fundamental principle. If George could have taken care of my family and me, and if he could have given my wife and me $500,000 and $250,000 of coverage at the same or lower premium as he gave us the $50,000 and $25,000 coverage, why didn't he? Wasn't it his responsibility as an honest and competent professional with integrity to do the very best job possible for my wife and me? And if he was not capable enough or honest enough to represent us properly the first time, why would I even entertain the possibility of doing business with him in the future?

He had stamped Ron's proposal with the "Not Invented Here," "Doesn't Put Money in My Pocket" stamp. He wasn't thinking about my family's interest. I came to the conclusion early on in my career, early on in my learning process, that if somebody was incompetent or dishonest with me, I wouldn't do business with that person, period; and that the person who was coming in with the proposal that made sense was the person who deserved to be treated with honesty and integrity. If I were to take Ron's recommendations and implement those recommendations with George, then I would not be dealing fairly with Ron. I had an ethical and moral obligation to deal with the person who had been honest and truthful with me. Ron deserved the business, because he was not looking out for himself; he was looking out for me and my family.

I still believe that today. I think that any time a professional has taken advantage of you or has failed to provide you with the best service available the first time around and then later, upon hearing somebody else's proposal, says, "I can do the same thing. And I've known you longer. I'm married to your old girlfriend, or I'm your brother-in-law, or I'm your neighbor. You should do the business with me; we play golf together," you should discount that person immediately. Anybody who uses those reasons to influence you is giving you further evidence of dishonesty and incompetence because what he or she is trying to do is to weasel in on somebody else's effort and take advantage of another person's time, talent and hard work.

I've encountered other situations in which advisors of mine used their "Not Invented Here" stamp and then tried to retain me as a client by playing on our relationship. For a while I listened to the original people, but I knew fundamentally that the honest thing to do was to give the business to the people who were really providing the greatest benefit to me and my family. My position is, "You had your opportunity and you should have taken care of me properly. You didn't. You failed me. You failed my family. You took unfair advantage of our relationship, and I'm not going to do business with you."

Your advisors need to be looking out for *your* best interest.

24

Show Me the Math

During George Bush's presidency, people waited and waited for the capital gains tax cut he kept talking about. In fact, every single time President Bush would say that he was going to reduce the capital gains taxes, the immediate response from the Democratic leadership in the House and the Senate was, in essence, "Forget it. We're not going to do that. We're not going to sacrifice the poor to reduce the taxes on the rich." In reality, there was no possibility of Bush's capital gains tax cut happening. But what did people do? They sat around and said, "George Bush promises he's going to reduce the capital gains tax rate. Therefore, I won't do anything at all. I'll just sit here and wait for President Bush's capital gains tax cut to go into effect."

It was very frustrating because it seemed that every six months or so President Bush would bring up this tax cut, and millions of people would then procrastinate on transactions they ought to have been making. They were waiting for this magical, mystical tax break to happen. And of course, it didn't happen.

So what happened to the people who were waiting for the capital gains tax break? The price of real estate declined dramatically during that time. Their real estate properties here in Southern California and a lot of other places throughout the country declined in value by as much as 50%. (That's one way to reduce your capital gains tax. However, it's not the method most people would choose.)

What did we do to combat this problem for our clients? We showed them the math. We said, "If President Bush's capital gains tax break goes through as outlined by the Bush administration with all the features in place, with nothing negotiated down, with no amendments, no changes, no resolutions, nothing attached to it, if it all goes through exactly as he is presenting it—and that would be obviously a tremendous case of wishful thinking—the actual reduction in capital gains taxes would be minimal. If your capital gains tax is $500,000, it would then be only $425,000." My experience with people is that if they don't want to pay $500,000 in capital gains tax, they don't want to pay $425,000 in capital gains tax either. Yet, their other advisors or they themselves did not sit down with a calculator and do the math.

Another example of ignoring the math would be the standard advice given by many professionals to their clients: "Just pay the tax. Get it over with. You only pay the tax once. Get it over with and get on with your life." Who are you likely to hear that from? Well, some real estate agents will tell you that when you're thinking about selling a property and you're concerned about the taxes. They'll say, "Well, you know, the property's a problem for you. You've got management headaches. Just get out of it. Just sell it. Pay the tax. Get on with your life. Deal with it."

Some accountants, attorneys and stock brokers will tell people the same thing. In a lot of cases they are motivated to see the deal happen because there's a substantial amount of commission, revenue and fees to be generated by selling or repositioning the assets, doing various analyses, crunching all the numbers, drafting documents and giving advice. So there can be some conflict of interest in the advice the client is receiving from the advisors.

Now, one way to determine whether advice is sound or not is to actually perform the mathematical analysis. In some of my seminars, I illustrate how you can take $350,000 you would have lost in capital gains tax, assume you could have earned an average of 8% over a life expectancy of 25 years, and discover that you have really lost $700,000 of income, not just $350,000 in taxes. Assuming interest is credited to your investments on a daily basis, and you're losing $700,000 in future income, you're paying for that tax not just once, but every day for 25 years. You're losing $700,000 in future income plus the ability to spend, enjoy or pass to the next generation $350,000 of net worth. The total loss is just over $1 million.

I was using this example in a seminar once when a fellow in the back of the room raised his hand. I called on him and he jokingly said, "Yeah, but if you don't live so long, it's not that bad." The point is, the advice to get it over with and move on is mathematically incorrect or, to be polite and give people the benefit of the doubt, incomplete at best. If you sat down and worked out the math, most people will say they don't want to pay. Intuitively, the right side of your brain knows that paying the tax and getting it over with doesn't feel right. What you have to do is put the left side of your brain to work and deal with the economic reality of crunching numbers. How can anyone possibly do any type of tax planning, financial planning or financial management without understanding the fundamental time value of money?

Basically, the time value of money principle means that it is better to use a tax deduction of a dollar today and save that dollar now rather than to spread that tax deduction over a period of years and take a full five or six years to recognize the full dollar. A dollar received five years from now historically has nearly always been worth less than a dollar today. So do what you can to get the dollar today. Do what you can to get the tax deduction today. Do what you can to take advantage of these things now, while you're alive, while you're able to do it. And make sure your advisors can show you the math to back up their recommendations or to refute the recommendations of others.

IV

*Wealth:
How to Manage It —
How to Avoid Being
Your Own Worst Enemy*

25

Performing Surgery Without a Scalpel

Sometimes it's not the advisors who are standing in the way of our happiness. Sometimes we impede our own progress. This section examines some of the traps you may set for yourself which can prevent you from reaching your goals.

Speaking as an advisor, I can tell you that sometimes we *can't* help our clients. They *won't let us* help them. They put so many restrictions on us that we can't do our jobs, or they have certain flawed perceptions which they will not adjust to meet reality. Sometimes it's as if certain clients are saying, "I want you to perform this surgery which will save my life, but I don't want you to use those scary, sharp-looking things because they look painful." And yet, there may be no other way to cure the problem than to use those scary, sharp-looking things.

Self-imposed restrictions take various forms. We'll discuss some of the most common problems clients cause for themselves in this section. Hopefully, you'll be able to recognize these problems and then avoid creating such problems for yourself.

Potential clients will hear me speak, meet with me, talk with me or read articles I have written, and say, "This sounds great. I know you're the person to help me. This is exactly what I've been looking for and what I need. I really want to do this." Then comes the inevitable question, "How much is it going to cost?"

My response is, "I don't know yet. Every situation is different. Because neither I nor my firm sells any products, we can be an unbiased third-party consultant working on your behalf.

Sometimes clients just won't let us help them.

We bill on a project basis as outlined in our retainer agreement. Once we have reviewed all of your information so that we can examine the whole picture, we'll quote you a fee outlined in a project agreement that we'll both sign." The clients say, "That sounds fair." When we receive a signed agreement and a retainer check, only then do we begin working on their case.

Understandably, clients want to know how much the strategic and tactical planning is going to cost. The truth is that it depends upon a couple of factors besides just the simplicity or complexity of their situations. Unfortunately it's hard to be blunt with the client and tell them exactly what those other factors are, but I'm going to tell you right now. It depends on you, the client, and it depends on your other advisors.

The personality and competency of the client's advisors contribute to the overall cost. For clients who have not selected an all-star team of advisors and who insist on using advisors who are not used to doing this type of planning or implementing these types of tactics, more time is involved in educating the advisors, so our cost goes up. The time and cost grow even larger if the advisors have difficult personalities, such as large egos and "Not Invented Here" stamps.

The other unknown cost factor is you, the client. How do you affect the cost? It takes time not only to review your situation and to make recommendations, it also takes time to explain the full situation and recommendations to you. Then it takes time for you to review the recommendations, ask questions, receive answers and make a decision. So, part of the cost depends on how quickly you learn and process information. Sometimes clients have to change their paradigms, so that their perceptions are aligned with reality. Some clients may have to change the way they look at the world in order to do this effectively. Some people are quick to make that adaptation and that change, and they become very effective very quickly. It costs less money for those people because there's less time involved. Others spend a great deal of time vacillating or objecting to the necessary changes they have to make. Some clients are very difficult to work with. Price is not a function of how much money the clients have, but of their personality, outlook, level of cooperation, speed of learning and retention. Price is a function of how well they can move ahead toward their dreams without getting bogged down in some of the traps we have discussed and others we will talk about in the following chapters.

26

Severing the Ties

I was consulting with a stock broker, Mike, about his mother. Mrs. M was in dire need of some sophisticated planning. However, she was insisting that we work with her existing attorney. The attorney had not been able to help the client resolve her problems even though she had represented her for many years and had had ample time to do so. For six weeks, I tried unsuccessfully to contact the attorney.

When I talked it over with Mike, he said, "Well, you know, the attorney's really sick. She's nearly 70 years old and has cancer." I said to Mike, "I'm sorry to hear that, but this attorney has not been able to help your mother for years now. If she could have, why didn't she? If this attorney were truly competent, she would have addressed these problems a long time ago for your mother. And, if she's as successful as your mother thinks she is, why is she still working at 70 years of age when she's trying to fight cancer?"

Because of her health situation, the attorney regularly left work or was not able to come in to work because she was in too much pain. That was unfortunate, and I felt bad for the attorney, but then why wasn't she welcoming some outside help to lighten her load and help the client? The real issue here was that the attorney was in denial about her health and about her inability to respond to her client's needs. She didn't want to benefit from hearing other opinions. She was not looking out for the best interest of the client, Mrs. M. Instead, the attorney was hoping her long-standing relationship with the client would stand up against outside representation.

When a client tells an advisor, "I want you to work with this particular attorney, accountant, stock broker, real estate agent, etc.," and that advisor won't cooperate, or worse, pretends to cooperate with no real intention of doing so, then obviously the job is made more difficult because of the increased hours it is going to take to work with that advisor. If the situation results in a stand-still in which the advisor just won't cooperate or is actually detrimental to the process, and the client can't sever the ties with that advisor, then the client is welcome to stay with that advisor and get the poor service and advice offered by that advisor. But they won't have our help.

At some point, you may have to sever more than professional ties. Relationships that are too emotionally biased can be detrimental to your goals. How fatal can it be when we don't sever these ties?

The Smiths were referred to me by a large banking institution. During my meeting with the couple, we had a wonderful discussion about what they wanted to accomplish, their goals and objectives. It seemed evident that what these people wanted to do would be beneficial not only for them and their family, but also for the community at large.

Mr. Smith had some health problems and needed to have angioplasty performed for the second time. In my business, I research and negotiate with a lot of charitable institutions on behalf of my clients. I had recently been to Northern California for a meeting with the board of directors of a large medical center. They introduced me to a technology that was in some cases vastly superior to angioplasty. I was amazed at the device they used and had a lengthy discussion at the medical center about this procedure.

I shared this information with Mr. Smith, and he was very enthusiastic. "That sounds incredible. I heard something about that technology becoming available in the future, but I didn't realize it was available already. Maybe this would be a good alternative for me."

I pointed out to him that one of the things the doctors had said was that it was not any more risky than angioplasty, and in their experience this treatment was far more effective. None of the patients who had undergone this procedure had needed to come back for a second treatment.

But then Mrs. Smith surprised me with her comment, "I appreciate you telling us about this, but we've already made the arrangements with one of the local hospitals here in town. I've been on their boards and committees for the last 25 years. We have a lot of friends over there."

Mr. Smith didn't see it that way. "This other treatment sounds very interesting, though. Maybe this is worth looking into," he said.

I offered to contact the medical center for him and put him in touch with a doctor so he could find out more about the procedure and whether or not it would be beneficial to him. I said, "This is obviously an important decision in your life, and you may want to do some research on this before you move ahead. At least get a second opinion."

Mrs. Smith became adamant that her husband was going to the local hospital because they had friends there and relationships there.

I explained that the medical center up north was a top-notch facility and with regard to this technology and treatment was far superior to the local hospital. After all, this could be a life and death situation. When we're faced with serious decisions, we should seek out the very best representation possible. You owe it to your family and yourself to do so, especially when you have the financial means to do so.

Mrs. Smith became more agitated. Mr. Smith suggested to his wife that I was merely pointing out the facts. The local hospital was not in the top 10, 20 or even 50 facilities known for this type of work. It was his life at risk; what was the harm in talking to the doctors at the medical center up north?

She replied, "It would be so embarrassing for me. How would I explain this to Dr. So-and-so and to Dr. So-and-so's wife? How would I explain this to other people on our committee if you go somewhere else for treatment?"

I was shocked that her pride and ego with respect to her friendships were more important to her than the health and well-being of her husband. The husband was absolutely crushed by her behavior. He asked me if I would set up a telephone conference with the doctors, and I did. Unfortunately, Mr. Smith did not keep the appointment.

About two weeks later, I was at a major medical center in Los Angeles which is one of the highest rated hospitals in the world for the type of treatment that Mr. Smith had needed. I was standing in line at the cafeteria with the executive director of their foundation when the head of cardiology walked into the room. He said hello to us, and I mentioned Mr. Smith's situation to him.

He said, "You know, we just had a patient who was brought in for tertiary care from that local hospital."

So I mentioned Mr. Smith by name and he said, "Yes, that's the fellow. He passed away this morning."

When I think about this incident, I reflect on how blinded people can be by their relationships, pride and ego. I don't know whether Mr. Smith would have done better had he gone to the Bay Area for the alternative treatment. Nobody knows if he would have survived. But what we do know is that Mr. Smith died without checking his options because of his wife's ties to the doctors and their wives at the local hospital.

This is how fatal not severing ties can be. I hope you won't make the same kind of mistake, with your health or your money.

27

It's Too Complicated

Nature tends to take the path of least resistance. Human nature is no exception. A complaint almost all professionals hear from clients is, "It's just too complicated." People tend to be prejudiced against unfamiliar things. And usually the older people become, the more resistant they are to changing from their comfortable positions. Sometimes anything different seems too complicated. However, by avoiding complication, we may also be avoiding the path which leads to our happiness and the fulfillment of our life's mission.

People who have created their own wealth took a risk somewhere along the line, but they often seem to forget it was a risk because now they're comfortable with it. For example, people who have made their fortunes in real estate may easily forget how they worried and debated over buying their first property. The acquisition of the second property was easier, and it became even easier as they acquired additional real estate assets.

Watch a couple buying their first rental property. The husband and wife will often have a great debate as to whether or not it's the right thing to do. The debate primarily centers around whether to put the money in the bank or in the credit union, or go way out on a limb and buy the property. Many people have gone out on that limb and bought that first property. Most of them will tell you that the stress, anxiety and frustration they felt seemed insurmountable. Their parents and other well-meaning "advisors" said, "You're crazy. You're putting your money into real estate?

You could lose the property. What if you lose your tenants and you can't rent it out? How are you going to make the mortgage payments?" Nonetheless, these people went forward and took the risk.

The assumed risk was calculated. Successful people tend to learn as much as they can reasonably learn and then take a calculated risk. Generally they're not gamblers. There's a clear distinction between gambling and risk-taking.

People will make the first investment, and then, if nothing earth-shatteringly terrible happens to them, their anxiety is eased. They become comfortable. Then investing in subsequent properties doesn't feel nearly as risky, because now they've been through the process; they have experience with it.

I look at myself as an example. Initially, in my first two or three business ventures, I had partners. Then I formed a firm on my own, Estate & Foundation Services, Inc. (EFS). It was my own thing; no partners, no shareholders. I had to progress to the point where I was willing to accept full responsibility and full accountability for my success or failure. That was the leap I had to make to go into business for myself; it had always seemed more comfortable to have partners or fellow stockholders who were bearing some of the risk, whereas with EFS it was all on my shoulders. Once EFS became successful, deciding to form my second company, what is now the Wright Company, was not as difficult because I was confident that I could make it go. But the greatest risk I assumed was the first time I decided to start my very own company.

Let's assume you and I became business partners. We formed a partnership and bought a single family home in the 1970s to be used as a rental property. Let's say we paid $35,000 for it. We put $5,000 down and assumed a $30,000 mortgage risk and hoped we could keep it occupied because it would take up all of our expendable cash each month to make the extra mortgage payment ourselves. Now in this hypothetical example, our income increased over time. The tax benefits from the real estate took effect and the risk did not seem as great as it once did. We also realized that it was not that difficult to keep the property rented out, and we learned the hard way about selecting quality tenants. As you and I learned to manage the various types of risk in that real estate, we became comfortable with them. Then, later on, we decided to either trade that property into something more significant, perhaps we did a 1031 exchange, or maybe we just bought another property and added to what we had in our portfolio.

Each time you and I decided to add to our portfolio, we assumed a higher level of risk. We had to deal with more tenants. We had a larger total debt to deal with. Eventually we could not, based on salary alone, support all of the debt. So when we made acquisitions, the debt had to be self-supported based upon the occupancy levels of the property. Let's assume that eventually you and I had 1500 rental units. The risk is, to all appearances, enormous. If you told people who owned no rental properties that in 20 years they would have 1500 tenants and a total debt of $8 million, they would absolutely freak out. Most people would run away and hide. They would not want to engage in that level of risk. However, if they could look ahead and say, "We might have $8 million in mortgages, but we have $25 million in equity," then the debt to equity ratio would make sense. Most people are willing to assume that kind of risk over 20 years. But it takes time. Generally speaking, success is a gradual thing; you grow into it!

However, many wealthy people have forgotten how they overcame complication in the process of acquiring their wealth. Many advisors are frustrated as they deal with clients who have been successful running a business, buying growth stocks or investing in real estate. Over a period of time, the various techniques that made the clients effective cease to be advantageous to them. In other words, the business needs to be sold, the growth stocks need to be converted into an income strategy, or the real estate no longer serves its best possible purpose with respect to family and personal goals. Yet some clients don't want to change the status quo even though they should— because they think the changes will be too complicated.

If the equity we have in growth positions is no longer in our best interest, we need to take a look around. We need to look for strategies, tactics and tools that will put our equity to better use. Eventually, we need to get into conversion strategies such as gifting and freezing tactics, capital gains tax avoidance, exchanges, etc., to move our equity from growth to income positions. The conversion process and strategies are complicated. So often clients will tell their advisors, "What you're telling me sounds interesting, but I don't really understand it. It's really complicated. I just want things to be simple." They take the position, "Maybe what I'm doing isn't in my best interest, but I'm used to it. I'm comfortable with it. And to me, it's simple. So therefore, I don't want to change."

You need to realize that you must act in your best interest, recognizing that times are going to change, investment markets are going to change, your needs are going to change. Therefore, you must be open to making changes because change is in your best interest. Failing to change is one of the worst things we can do because that means we fail to progress, we fail to grow, and we cease to be effective and efficient in managing our affairs.

The curse of wealth is complication. The more money you have, the more complication there is in controlling and maintaining your wealth. Just because you're used to it doesn't mean that it's easy; it just means you've gotten good at it. What you are doing today is extremely complicated compared to what you were doing 10 or 15 years ago. Even if you think it's not more complicated, it is. The rules that we lived by when we initially started have changed. What was relatively uncomplicated with regard to government regulation, for example, has become infinitely more regulated and therefore more complicated. You may think what you're doing now is easy, but 20 years ago it would have been overwhelming to you. You've grown into a level of complication that you never imagined you could handle.

If we look at business as an example, the number of regulations imposed upon businesses 15, 20 or 30 years ago was significantly less than today. Each one of today's regulations often carries with it hundreds or thousands of pages of complicated detail. Therefore, it complicates our business. Over a period of time, we develop a management philosophy and strategy for dealing with those changes. We may not take the time to write them down or say, "Here's what changes we have to make," or "Here's our policy for dealing with these changes," but we do develop a style for dealing with the changes. Things around us change, and we adapt. If we don't adapt to those changes, we'll go out of business.

Our advisors may be able to explain the Americans With Disabilities Act, as an example, and the impact upon our real estate holdings or our business as a result of that regulation, but that's thousands of pages of regulation. How many business owners actually read it? All they want to know is, "How does it affect my business?" It's very complicated, but they should have good advisors who can condense the information, simplify it and get to the bottom line.

Imagine that you are my client. I've explained some strategies to you and provided you with several options to achieve your goals. You're thinking, "Oh boy, this is really complicated stuff. What I'm doing now is easy and I'm used to it." One of the recommendations I've made to you is a Section 664 trust. This is a tax-exempt trust. There are issues such as unrelated business income taxes which can invalidate the trust for tax-exempt purposes for any given year. Just understanding unrelated business income and the tax consequences is a point of discussion that can go on for hours at professional conferences and seminars. I have to convince you that there's an advantage for you in changing. The grass is, in fact, greener over here than where you currently are. But your experience has been, "Well, the grass always looks greener, but when I get over there it may not be any better or even as good as where I was before." So there's more to this than the math. Perhaps the math may look greener, but you can't always make the comfort level look so attractive.

In our role playing, I would say to you, "The curse of wealth is complication. I know this is a very difficult thing. I know a lot of the tactics I've been talking to you about, 664 trusts, private foundations, family partnerships, etc., are complicated issues. But you know, while those things are complicated, you should be thankful we're not talking about Internal Revenue Code section 408 trusts because a section 408 trust is very, very complicated. I'll throw a couple of examples out at you. You may not think this is relevant, but I think it is in the broad base of our discussion."

So I continue while you listen with increasing feelings of anxiety, "Under Internal Revenue Code section 408, if you want to create a trust that qualifies as a tax-advantaged trust, which most people are looking for when they get involved in a 408 trust, they don't realize that there's an enormous amount of fiduciary responsibility that goes along with IRC 408. It would be very difficult for an individual person with a background in real estate, investments or business to just suddenly jump into this mode of expertise in fiduciary responsibility as it relates to section 408. The filing and the reporting on a large 408 trust, I would say any trust over $100,000 or even $50,000, can have a lot of complication depending upon how many investment holdings there are and how often the reports and status come in on those investments. . . ."

I go on to outline the technical elements of the 408 trust:

• Principles of tax deferral under section 408

• Filing and reporting responsibilities of the holder

• Limits on gross earnings contributions

• Private letter rulings devoted to 408 issues

By the time I've elaborated all these points, your eyes have completely glazed over. Then I ask, "Does this sound attractive to you based on what I've told you about it?"

Your response would typically be, "It sounds incredibly complicated, and I don't want to have anything to do with it." The funny thing is, as complicated and as difficult as it sounds, you probably have a section 408 trust right now without even knowing it. You see, the more common name for that type of trust is an Individual Retirement Account, or an IRA.

Whether you know it or not, you have been engaged in a very, very complicated thing. But here's the difference: It wasn't complicated for you personally because IRAs have been packaged in a way that makes them user-friendly. Perhaps all you had to do was fill out a very brief form down at the bank or at the broker's office. If you look at any type of qualified plan, IRA, pension, KEOGH or self-employed pension account, you will find that they have tremendously complicated details. But the way they're packaged to consumers makes them seem simple. The lesson is that very complicated things can be presented in a way to make them quite practical.

The decision-making process should be the same regardless of our perceived notion of the complexity of the strategy. You should weigh the advantages and disadvantages. You focus on the benefits, tax savings and long-term possibilities. And you say, "This all makes sense to me." The disadvantages which are demonstrated to you with IRAs are not the complicated fiduciary issues, but rather, "If you put the money in, there's a penalty if you pull it out early." So you look at that and you say, "That's no big deal. I wouldn't want to pull that money out early. This is a retirement account. I don't want that money until I'm ready to retire anyway." You can live with that downside because of all the advantages.

No one really sits down with you and tells you the whole story. They don't disclose to you all of the details and all of the nuances. They may even tell you, "You can be in control of this IRA and you can pick all of the investments you want." This is what is called in technical terms a self-directed IRA, meaning you retain the right to direct the investments.

I've gone through this section 408 scenario with attorneys and accountants, and they say, "I've never heard of a 408. It sounds like it's got some nice features to it, but it is terribly complicated. My clients would never go for that." In point of fact, their clients go for it all the time. They've gone for it themselves, because most of them have IRAs. Yet they don't recognize the IRA as a 408 trust when it is laid out with all the details because normally it's presented in a simple package. "I never realized it was that complicated," they'll say.

You can approach strategies, tactics and planning as you do an IRA. You can retain the right of control and self-direct your investments, but dictate or delegate all of the less favorable, less attractive points to someone who possesses that expertise. You can retain the right to hire and fire the advisors, and therefore maintain the control that's important to you, but you don't have to get caught up in the complicated stuff.

You're already doing complicated things. These strategies, tactics and changes may appear complicated, but it doesn't have to be any more difficult than what you're dealing with now. It's just difficult in your own mind because you're unfamiliar with it, just as everything else was when you first got into it. You must not allow yourself to be overcome with the fear of perceived complication just because something is new to you.

When you first started out, perhaps you had little or no money. You also had very little financial complication. Then, as you started doing more and more, you were engaged in complicated decisions. Just to become wealthy, you have to be engaged in complicated issues. You must take risks. You must gain knowledge and ability. You must evolve as the world changes. Any time we're going to change something, we're going into the unknown. We'll start looking for some reason why we don't have to make that change because we're so comfortable where we are. We need to make sure that our human nature isn't ruling us. We have to be able to master ourselves and master human nature in order to be truly successful in anything.

When things become uncomfortable, we want to stop. If we're training to win a marathon or a 100-mile bicycle race, we're going to go through a great deal of discomfort. Our pain threshold will increase as we go through it, but we have to fight human nature in order to do it. We have to struggle and continue to grow in managing our wealth as well. So if you want to achieve your goals, you're going to have to make changes and tackle some issues and implement some strategies that may seem complicated, just as you've conquered complication before.

Don't give up by saying, "It's too complicated," and thus fail to progress toward your goals. Don't cheat yourself, your family and your mission in life because of a little discomfort. A certain amount of discomfort can be your friend. No pain; no gain. This applies universally throughout our lives. Emotionally, spiritually and physically we cannot move forward without experiencing discomfort. The more evolved we become, the more uncomfortable we are with the status quo. Show me a person comfortable with the status quo, and I can guarantee you that person isn't growing and lacks a profound sense of purpose.

28

But I Grew Up on That Property

Investments are neutral. Stock prices just do what they do. Real estate just does what it does. Your equity position is the critical thing to focus on. Is your equity doing what you really want it to do? Are you effectively using it to live your perfect calendar?

We have to separate ourselves from the emotional aspects of owning a particular piece of property or particular stocks. They are inanimate tools. Assets are supposed to be working for us. Are they empowering us to accomplish our goals? We need to have the ability to re-focus our attention so that we look at our decisions intelligently and logically rather than from a purely emotional standpoint. Usually there's going to be some emotion involved; we must learn to recognize and balance it. Perhaps it's best to look at it this way: It's fine to be emotional about our goals, our mission or our legacy, but it is very unwise to be emotional about the tools we employ to get there. The tools are merely a means to an end. As times change, so will the effectiveness of a given tool. An incalculable amount of opportunity, benefit, good work and even peace of mind has been lost due to some people's tendency to form emotional attachments to or fears about inanimate objects like investments and assets.

"It's been in the family for generations. It means so much to the whole family." This is a comment my colleagues and I hear all the time. Nearly 100% of the time it is a sincere statement. But since such commentary is totally emotional, it is mathematically and financially irrelevant. Furthermore, usually no one but the speaker feels so strongly about the "family farm." After the person who makes that statement is out of the picture, the property will almost always be sold. The heirs would nearly always rather have the cash. Even in those rare cases in which the heirs would like to have the property, they may be forced to liquidate in order to pay the taxes and/or distribute equity to other heirs who want the cash. Keep in mind also that heirs' spouses and children will have a lot of influence on such matters, be it directly or indirectly. Most of them have no significant emotional attachment whatsoever to the "family farm."

Greta was a nice woman with a good heart. She had two homes, one in the Southwestern desert for the winter and one in the Rocky Mountains for the summer. Her net worth was approximately $5 million. Nearly everything she had was tied up in her two homes and $3.8 million in stock in one company. She lived off the dividends and just barely had enough income to get by.

One day she got tired of the stress and called her financial advisor and asked, "What can I do to increase my income?" She wanted more cash flow to travel and contribute to her favorite causes. Her financial advisor, Mark, called me with the referral. Her CPA, her attorney, Mark and I spent several months working out the options and details of her strategic plan so we could accomplish her goals. We even had discussions with the charities that were important to her. Everything was ready to go. The documents were all drawn up to everyone's satisfaction. Greta would accomplish every goal and desire she had.

But then it happened. She called Mark and said she just couldn't sell any of the stock. You see, her grandfather had started a farm. Her father ran the farm and then traded the family corporation stock (which held the farm) to a large, publicly traded farming conglomerate. Greta was concerned that if she now sold the stock, she would be disloyal to her father and grandfather. Mark suggested that although he had not known either the father or grandfather, it seemed to him that they would want her to be happy. He pointed out that since she wouldn't be selling all of the stock anyway, she might hang the new stock certificate in a frame in her home.

What did Greta do? She had incurred thousands of dollars in professional fees. All of her personal and legacy goals were finally within reach. She could be fulfilled. But instead, she did nothing. In a fit, she lashed out at Mark and said to me, "Who does he think he is? He didn't know my father. How would he know what my father wanted for me?" Greta was unreasonably emotional and unreachable. What missed opportunities! What missed advantages for her personally and for the community! How could this happen with stock in a company where Greta knew none of the executives, not a single board member, no one? How could an otherwise intelligent, reasonable adult act so irresponsibly and immaturely?

Unfortunately, Greta is not alone in her stubbornness. I assure you that many people behave similarly and that the results are the same—missed opportunities, lost benefits and unfulfilled lives.

Have you ever known anyone whose parents or spouse said, "Honey, don't ever sell this stock (building, farm, business, etc.). Whatever you do, just don't part with this"? Such advice is given all the time, and it is *always* wrong, eventually. It is advice issued without consideration for market timing, changing tax codes or reality, and it is intellectually bankrupt.

Many elderly widows live under unnecessary financial stress because of such irresponsible attachments. They feel that if they were to part with a certain asset, they would somehow be disrespectful or disloyal to the deceased spouse. So here is a clue to end the insanity: *You can't take it with you when you go! So make it work for you while you're alive.*

Once you are gone, you cannot time the markets, watch the economy or pay attention to an ever-changing tax code. Would anybody in their right mind pay for financial advice from a person with no concept of market conditions, tax law or the economy? Absolutely not! Dead people do not have a clue about such things. Therefore, their advice beyond the date of their departure is, shall we say, without merit. And, if they love you, wouldn't they want you to be able to use the wealth to make you happier and better off?

When we leave this world, we not only leave behind our temporal assets, we leave behind our legacy, our attitude, our deeds and perhaps, if we have any, our wisdom. If our parents and spouses are not wise enough to realize the impact of dysfunctional comments and attitudes, perhaps this chapter will help you to be wiser than they.

In summary I offer only this: Don't take specific microtactical, asset management or tax advice from dead guys.

29

Putting on Your Overalls

We are all in business. Whether you work for somebody else, are self-employed or even retired, you have business to conduct. There comes a time when you must focus on managing your equity and structuring your wealth rather than just concentrating on the day-to-day details of managing your business, real property, stock portfolio, etc. Your equity needs to become your business. Let me give you an example of what can happen when you neglect to change your focus.

One morning, I met with an attorney named Bob. Bob was looking forward to introducing me to his client Fred that afternoon because he had been unable to get Fred to pay attention to the wealth management issues he needed to consider. Fred was sitting on about $15 million of equity and was paying Bob to help him manage this $15 million. The attorney knew it was his responsibility in representing his client to get him at least to look at the strategies he and I were discussing. Based on our calculations that morning, Bob thought we could save Fred $4-5 million in unnecessary taxes.

When we returned to the office after lunch, Bob's receptionist told us that Fred had called to cancel the meeting. Bob called Fred to find out what was more important than saving $5 million of his hard-earned wealth. Fred was no longer at home, but his wife told Bob the reason for the cancellation: "One of our neighbors called to say he's got a bunch of apple hulls on the ground. Fred went to pick up the apple hulls with the pickup truck so he could bring them back and feed them to the cattle."

The attorney thanked the wife for the information and hung up the phone. He was livid. He said, "You know, we're trying to help this guy. We could save him $5 million. We could help this guy redirect his finances in a way that would be tremendously advantageous for him and his family. But what's he doing instead? He's shoveling apple hulls to feed to his cattle."

The cattle probably appreciated the apple hulls, but that should not have been Fred's focus. Fred had a bunch of laborers working on his farm. In terms of the cost of time, for 40 bucks he could have had somebody go over to his neighbor's place and take care of the apple hulls. But instead, this guy put on his overalls and grabbed his shovel. He's got a $15 million equity position which he should be managing. What was he doing instead? Shoveling apple hulls.

Fred had hired Bob to help manage his $15 million of equity, and Bob took his responsibility seriously. His job was to help protect this man's $15 million of equity. He had set up a meeting to deal with Fred's problems, and Fred sabotaged everything to go shovel apple hulls.

I've got a business to run. If I were to sit in front of a computer and hunt and peck to type my own letters, I would be stupid. If I had stockholders to worry about, I would be doing a tremendous disservice to those stockholders. Fred did not realize he was hurting his family. So he saved himself $40 in labor cost? He cost himself and his family $5 million in equity. We need to realize that we must treat our equity like a business. In fact, it ought to be our most important business.

What is your focus? If you're used to "putting on your overalls" in the morning and going out there and digging ditches, building buildings, making widgets or whatever it is you do, then you need to re-think or challenge your focus. There comes a time when it is irresponsible for you to forego strategic planning and equity management for day-to-day tasks. It's irresponsible to your stock holders. It's irresponsible to your mission in life. It's irresponsible to your family. Wake up. Pay attention. You are in business for yourself. *You are your business.* Go out there and do something effective with it.

If you have advisors who are trying to fulfill their roles and protect and preserve your wealth, cooperate with them. That's what you are paying them for. Don't say, in effect,

"I've got to go shovel apple hulls." It's absolutely irresponsible not to manage your equity. Yet, many people don't want to stop doing the day-to-day tasks and deal with the more rewarding issues of managing and protecting their wealth. Part of it is habit; they're used to doing the day-to-day routine. But I think for a lot of people, they're blocking out what they need to deal with. It's *easier* for them to pursue the path of least resistance. It's certainly more comfortable, convenient and easier to, figuratively speaking, put on the overalls and shovel apple hulls for the afternoon than to go to your attorney's office and sit and talk with some "guys in suits" on complicated financial matters you don't understand or don't want to understand.

If you're a basketball player and you know basketball, you'd probably rather go dribble a basketball and shoot a few hundred shots than go deal with business outside your area of expertise or comfort. But at some point in time, you're not playing basketball anymore and you're thinking, "Geez, I don't have as much money as I'd like to have," or "I've lost some money," or maybe somebody ripped you off and stole money from you. But, hey, when you had the chance to deal with those details, you didn't want to do it.

Too many people get so lost in the "game" that they overlook or neglect the true business of overall macro wealth management and/or strategic planning. Sometimes people sacrifice their personal relationships with spouses, children and friends for the sake of the "game." Wake up, the "game" is not who you are. You are not a manufacturer, attorney, developer or ball player. You are a spiritual, physical, emotional being capable of so much more than the "game."

So don't sit there and say, "The government's going to take millions of my hard-earned wealth away. This is terrible. Somebody's got to do something about this." You have to do something about it. You have to pay attention to it. You have to get the right people around you and when those people around you say, "Listen, you need to deal with this," you've got to have the discipline and maturity to recognize that you can't go shovel apple hulls today. You've got to go deal with the really important issues. Ask yourself, "What's more important to me? The day-to-day management of shoveling apple hulls and feeding the cattle, which I can delegate to other people, or the management of my $15 million of equity? What's the most responsible thing I can do with my time, talents and resources today?" It's a prioritizing process that we all have to go through.

Many good advisors are frustrated. They take their jobs seriously. What's going to happen to Bob the attorney down the road when Fred dies and the family says, "None of these issues were taken care of. Bob, you're supposed to be his advisor. Why didn't you take care of these issues? It's all your fault." Bob's defense is going to be, "I tried to get Fred to deal with this, but he was busy shoveling apple hulls."

30

Analysis Paralysis

Many people find it difficult to plan because of the constant change we face every day. This state of flux can be very intimidating, and the result of this intimidation is most often a lack of action. For some reason, people often behave as though they can just remain where they are, ignore the changes going on around them and somehow escape harm. This is like a small child pulling the covers over his head to escape the monster in the closet. A person lying in bed with the covers pulled over his head makes an easy meal for the bogeyman.

Once we acknowledge that things are going to be constantly changing, and that we can't just sit by and do nothing and expect to win, we can begin to gather information and make decisions. However, we have to watch out for a mental condition which can be fatal to our success— analysis paralysis.

Considering the abundance of data available in this age of information, it is unlikely that a person will have *all* of the facts on any subject before making a decision. You could spend your whole life gathering information and never arrive at a decision. This is what many experts refer to as "analysis paralysis." Instead of accomplishing their goals, some people are dragging their situations out to the point where they may end up dying before they actually implement any necessary strategies or tactics. They say, "This is a really important decision. I have to consider all of the variables before I make a move." That's true, but only to a point. Therein lies the trap.

One of my clients, Joanne, definitely had analysis paralysis. This very nice lady had been in the real estate business for more than 20 years. During that time, she had followed the advice she gave to clients and purchased numerous properties herself. Eventually her properties went up in value. The problem was that as the properties got older, they needed more repairs and other attention. Of course, as the properties got older, so did Joanne. She no longer had the desire or energy to deal with the headaches of property management. Her short-term goals were to get out of real estate and invest and diversify the proceeds between the bank and her stock broker. She just wanted dividend and interest checks in the mailbox each month without all of the real estate hassles she'd been dealing with for the last 20 years.

Because Joanne's net worth was nearly all tied up in this real estate, she was facing a very emotional as well as financial decision. She would be changing her entire lifestyle. Joanne just wanted to focus on short-term goals and ignore the macro issues of the lifestyle change. This is all too common with people who fall into the analysis paralysis trap.

Joanne had attended one of my seminars and decided she wanted to talk with me. We had a meeting to discuss her goals, plans and problems. She wasn't thrilled with my insistence that she look at the macro issues. She did not want to share her "personal" information. She just wanted me to look at the numbers associated with converting her real estate into diversified, low-risk, income-producing investments without paying any capital gains taxes. She didn't want to do a real estate exchange because she wanted to "retire" from the headaches. She wanted to avoid the capital gains tax a conventional real estate sale would trigger. An installment sale would not reduce her risk or allow adequate diversification of equity. These are all straightforward and common issues for my firm to deal with. There are many solutions to choose from to fulfill these objectives. Our firm could easily have helped Joanne.

Of course there must be a "but" in every situation, or it wouldn't be worth telling the story. I had to reject the case not because I couldn't help Joanne, *but* because Joanne would not let me really help her. She could not understand the important dynamics associated with the process of change. We parted company on friendly terms, and I invited her to call me if she realized the importance of looking at the big picture and the need to move ahead and make decisions.

Three years later, Joanne called. She told me how she had explored *"all"* the different options and still had not done a thing. While she was stuck in analysis paralysis, her real estate holdings had declined approximately $1 million in value. Joanne was sufficiently humbled by these regrettable losses. She was now teachable. It is unfortunately true that many people must personally absorb a significant loss in order to become teachable. We agreed to take her case since she was now willing to consider the macro dynamics associated with the planning.

Of course, it still wasn't smooth sailing with Joanne. Analysis paralysis is a behavior that runs deep and is hard to cure. First, we had to review the many pages of "free" analysis she had gathered from various salespeople along with some she had performed herself. All of this analysis was flawed or incomplete. Some people try to pass off such mistakes by saying, "Well, you get what you pay for. All this stuff was free." I beg to differ. All that "free" analysis combined with just enough arrogance, pride and ignorance cost Joanne more than $1 million as her property declined in value while she took no action.

As we worked to help her reach her goals, she would sometimes become annoyed with me and let me know that her insurance agent and CPA were more "agreeable" than I was. When this would come up, I'd smile and ask, "Did you hire me to help you or to agree with you?"

Sometimes people's greed can cause them to get stuck in analysis paralysis. They're afraid that, if they make a decision and implement a tactic, someday something better will come along and somehow they'll lose out. Analysis paralysis can really cloud our thinking. For example, one of my clients, Mark, was considering a charitable trust. The payout period of that trust would be his lifetime or 20 years, whichever lasted longer. That was how long he would receive an income from the earnings of the trust. He was concerned that if he died six months after creating the trust, somehow he'd be losing out on a whole bunch of money he would have received if he had lived longer. However, what he was failing to see was that whether he would have received that income or not was irrelevant because, after all, he would be dead. It was like saying, "If I die sooner than I'd like, I won't get to take that trip to Europe I'm planning." Well, that's true. If you die before your trip, you won't get to go to Europe. But isn't it worse never even to plan the trip you want to take? If you never plan the trip, you'll really never get there. You have to implement a plan if you want to reach your goals.

In Mark's case, we had constructed a plan to accomplish all of his and his wife's objectives. Yet Mark was always trying to wring one more cent out of the plan. Just as we would be ready to implement his plan, he would hear of another twist that he would want to explore even though we'd explain that the tactic he was proposing wouldn't accomplish his goals. All he did by persisting in his analysis paralysis was further complicate matters and put off the implementation of his plan to such a point where he and/ or his wife were likely to die before reaching their goals. If that happened, then they'd be unable to take advantage of all the things that were presently available to them.

How do you know when you have analysis paralysis? Here are a few telltale signs.

- You start redoing the calculations provided by your advisors.

- You attend more than three seminars (without free food) on a specific subject.

- You decide your advisors' analysis is not enough and you start performing your own analysis of the situation.

- You become obsessed with getting *all* of the facts before you make a decision.

- You realize after two years that you still haven't actually implemented anything.

Each year I meet at least a few people who are suffering from some type of mental condition which inhibits their progress or fulfillment. We've talked about ego, pride and ignorance, but you must also consider that some people have genuine mental disorders. In some cases, it's necessary to include a psychologist or psychiatrist as part of an advisory team. Sometimes the plan for that client must include more than financial and tax strategies or tactics. I have worked with clients who could not proceed until receiving medication or psychological treatment. Sometimes substance abuse rears its ugly head and must be dealt with. You will not achieve maximum effectiveness or true happiness until you overcome such obstacles or addictions.

31

Tough Love

Some financially successful people tend to surround themselves with "yes" people. "Yes advisors" say yes to everything their clients suggest and everything they want to do, sometimes even when it's not in the best interest of the clients. In the worst cases, what the client wants is illegal, immoral or unethical, but the "advisors" pursue it anyway. These advisors are either too afraid of losing the client, or are so greedy they don't want to lose the revenue that comes from the client. Basically a lot of the "yes advisors" are just so happy to have this big client that they pretty much do anything the client wants even if it's not in the client's best interest and even if they know better. They're so intimidated or frightened by the client that they won't just come right out and tell the client the truth. We've all heard the fairy tale of the emperor's new clothes, in which the emperor thinks he's wearing beautiful garments and it takes the truthfulness of a young boy to tell him he's really naked. I think it's incumbent upon clients to be mature enough to realize that they don't want to be like the emperor. Wise clients want to know the truth.

The experience that comes to mind along these lines is Jake's story. Jake had surrounded himself with attorneys, accountants and real estate people whom he had known for years. Jake really fancied himself a very knowledgeable fellow when it came to real estate; after all, he and his family had owned real estate in the Los Angeles area for many years. Therefore, Jake was an expert on real estate—in his mind anyway.

A couple of years before I met Jake and his wife, Jake had put a piece of property on the market. In a short period of time, his real estate agent had found several potential buyers, one of which was a large foreign corporation wanting to build a corporate office and factory headquarters. The company had offered $12 million cash for this property. Jake felt that the property was worth more than $12 million. He had not gathered any evidence supporting that figure, he just *felt* that it was worth more. The real estate agent didn't want to argue with Jake because—what the heck—if they could find a buyer for more money, well, then, there would be more commission for the real estate company.

If Jake had been more in touch with his own level of knowledge and market realities, he would have jumped on that $12 million offer and been happy to have the cash. But he wasn't paying attention to the national and world economies. He didn't heed the warnings of the experts who were predicting that real estate prices would begin to decline dramatically. And his advisors weren't telling him this piece of bad news; they weren't deviating from the "yes" roles they had established for themselves.

Instead of taking the offer, Jake thought, "The property's worth more than this offer. We're having some problems making the insurance payments and property taxes, so we'll borrow money against our apartment building." A couple of years later, they borrowed money against their house, too, and before they knew it, all of their other properties were highly encumbered. They couldn't meet the debt service and were literally on the verge of foreclosure on their apartment building and in jeopardy of losing their personal residence as well. Jake was irate by the time I met him through his estate planning specialist, Bill, with whom I had worked on quite a number of other cases.

Bill introduced Jake and me and told Jake that if anybody could fix this situation, it would be my company. His attorneys, accountants, real estate agents, life insurance people, stock brokers, bankers, all of the people he had experience with were unable to find any solutions for him. As soon as I met Jake, I recognized the biggest problem in all of this was Jake himself and his attitude that he knew everything.

Of course if you asked Jake, it was George Bush, Ronald Reagan and Congress who were the cause of his problems. All of his problems were somebody's fault, but they certainly weren't his own fault. And every time there was a meeting to discuss possible options for fixing the problem, Jake would go into a tirade and explain how it was everybody's fault.

We worked through a series of options, and finally we came up with a set of tactics everybody agreed to, including Jake. But when the time came to execute the necessary documents to put the tactics into place, Jake began to rant about how it was everybody's—but not his own—fault that the property was now appraised at only $7 million. It looked as if he wasn't going to execute the necessary documents and implement the tactics after all. His wife was on the verge of an emotional collapse because of all the troubles, and she was contemplating divorcing him at least in part because of his arrogance and rudeness.

Jake needed a dose of tough love. I pointed out to him that he could blame Reagan, he could blame Bush, he could blame Congress, he could blame everybody and anybody that he wanted to, but that was not going to improve his personal net worth. Furthermore, Jake could go into foreclosure on his house and his apartment building and ultimately lose the land as well, move into a cardboard box somewhere in Tijuana, Mexico, and tell all the rest of the homeless people living in boxes that he used to have a net worth of $16 million dollars. Some of them might even believe him, but that wouldn't really be much consolation. He'd still be living in a box in Tijuana. So he could whine and complain about how he felt it was everybody else's fault, but that wasn't going to change his circumstances. He needed to implement this strategic plan and accompanying tactics if he was going to salvage anything.

He looked at me with a rather shocked expression and said, "I can't believe you just said that."

So I calmly and lovingly continued, "Furthermore, Jake, you may not be the real estate expert you like to think you are. You had a $12 million cash offer for this property—before you encumbered the other properties and put yourself in jeopardy. Had you taken the time and trouble to research the market conditions, you would have discovered that virtually any objective, third-party resource was predicting a dramatic recession in the real estate market."

When people think they are experts, they should ask themselves, "Would someone hire me as an expert in this particular area?" There was nobody anyplace, anywhere willing to hire Jake as a real estate expert. Jake wouldn't have hired himself as a real estate expert if he had sat down and looked at the facts. His overestimation of his abilities, his arrogance, pride and ignorance had cost him many millions of dollars and could have cost his family's financial security and future. If he did not go ahead and execute the tactics that everyone had concluded were the best options for him to pursue, he would lose the roughly $7 million of net worth he had remaining. He would be broke.

Jake was furious. He told me that he had never been so insulted in his entire life. He got up and said to his wife, "Come on, we're leaving."

She looked at him and said, "If you walk out that door, I'm divorcing you and our relationship is over." Considering that they had been married for better than 30 years at that point, it was a very powerful statement.

"Jake," she said, "you are completely wrong. You have screwed this up from the very beginning, and you're about to screw it up even worse. We've hired these people to help us solve our problems. They've been able to work an absolute miracle here to help us save $7 million of the assets that we're going to lose a week from now if we don't do this. And you're ready to get up and walk out the door and waste all their time and energy? You ought to be ashamed of yourself. You're prideful and arrogant, and I'm not going to take it anymore."

Incredulously he asked, "What are you saying?"

She simply said, "You sit down and sign those papers, Jake."

Not only was I practicing "tough love" on Jake, so was his wife. She knew that he needed to hear the truth, as painful as it might be for her to say it and as painful as it was for him to hear it. Thus, she was able to salvage the net worth they had remaining.

This couple is now among our strongest and most avid supporters and sometimes make themselves available as references for potential clients. They know what it's like to go to the brink of financial ruin and be saved at the last possible moment. There are a lot of people out there who to one degree or another have this kind of problem: a profound arrogance and a tremendous overestimation of their knowledge and ability with regard to financial markets. They're just so grossly mistaken that it takes tough love—someone to stand up and tell them the truth—to save them from financial disaster.

Such arrogant personalities tend to compound the problem by surrounding themselves with "yes people," who actually sit there and listen to their tirades and put up with their immature, inane behavior. They don't recognize how detrimental this is. I hope this story will help you and the people you care about become more open-minded and less prideful. I've come to the conclusion over the years that if you combine arrogance and pride with ignorance, you have a volatile mixture. If you throw in a few "yes men," the situation becomes dangerous. Somebody has to step in with tough love and truth-telling to save the day.

It's important to have advisors who care enough about us as individuals to tell us the truth, who have enough concern about our best interest to put their own interest on the line, who will come right out and tell us, when we're wrong, that we don't know what we're talking about and to knock it off. It seems that the wealthier, more powerful and older we become, the more crotchety, stubborn and determined we are. Perhaps your "Rate Your Knowledge" experience in Chapter 14 will prove helpful in reducing this problem for you. That exercise has proven invaluable time and time again in helping people recognize their level of proficiency (or lack thereof) and the fact that it will take a team comprised of at least "level 7s" or above to help us win the game. "Rate Your Knowledge" is a favorite tool of spouses, business partners and heirs to help someone gain the perspective they need to be more effective.

32

Price Versus Cost

Two couples were sitting in a meeting. One couple was worth $35 million and one couple was worth $2 million. The couple worth $2 million walked out of the meeting and said, "The price for all that brain power is too rich for me." The other couple, worth $35 million, left the same meeting and said, "We can't afford *not* to hire those people." It wasn't a matter of money, the people worth $2 million could definitely have afforded the help. It was their paradigm that kept them from getting the expertise they needed, and it was their paradigm that would keep them at $2 million and bar them from ever reaching $35 million.

Price and cost are not the same. Price is what you pay today. Cost equals the long-term effect of what you did or did not do. The price of any advice should be weighed against the long-term cost, benefits or overall savings. Earlier I mentioned a lady in Palm Springs who did not want to do her strategic planning because the "price" was too high, yet her inaction was going to "cost" her estate $12 million in estate and other taxes. Was the $15,000, or $50,000, or $100,000 or even $200,000 that she might have had to pay to get her wealth structured correctly too much to pay in order to save $12 million?

Should you be looking for a bargain when it comes down to setting and achieving your goals and/or managing your wealth? "My alma mater said they'll set up my charitable trust and manage the money for free." "My son-in-law is a financial planner, and he said he'll do my estate plan and life insurance at a fraction of the cost others would charge." Have you ever heard or made those kinds of statements before?

My response to statements like those is, "Have you ever heard the phrase 'You get what you pay for'?" Price is only an issue when we fail to understand real value.

This story by general contractor Allen Gorin comes from a local newspaper:

There was an elderly plant maintenance supervisor who made his hydro-electric plant hum like a well-oiled machine. For years, this intricately equipped monument to man's technological genius functioned so smoothly that hardly any members of the corporate board even knew there was a supervisor. Then came his retirement. Gold-watch time, the moment the quiet janitor from the school of hard knocks stepped aside for a younger, credentialed professional.

Shortly thereafter, there was a malfunction at the plant. Whatever it was, the entire operation was soon at a standstill. Neither the CEO, plant managers, or the new, credentialed professional had the faintest idea what to do about it. Every hour of down-time translated to $5,800 in lost revenue. Finally, someone thought to call the retired plant maintenance supervisor and ask him to come fix it. He obliged, donned his cap, and returned to his former workplace.

Within minutes of being briefed on the circumstances, he walked over to a huge turbine, tapped it with a pipe wrench, and everyone watched as the plant started back up. The old man left and the only trace of his presence was a handwritten bill he left behind. The total of the bill was $1,001. He had itemized the bill as follows: (1) Time to fix problem (five minutes)—$1.00, (2) Knowledge and experience accumulated over a lifetime to know how to fix problem—$1,000.00.

Was it worth it? Should he have worked up a sweat and made the repair seem more difficult in order to justify the bill? The CEO knew the true cost of having the plant shut down and he knew the value of results. He paid the bill and had no trouble sleeping that night.

I don't mean to imply that you should pay an exorbitant fee for an acceptable result. Clearly, the fee should be in line with what the market will bear. But what we need to understand is that what seem to be top-dollar fees can be, in reality, quite worth the price (if not downright inexpensive) when measured against the results, benefits or savings they bring.

Expertise is the combination of knowledge and experience. Expertise is worth the price when it produces the desired results. Would you want your brain surgeon reading from a textbook during the operation? Do you want your attorney to charge for research time when a more qualified attorney has implemented and defended the strategy or tactic successfully numerous times? Services you thought you were getting for less may end up costing you many times what true specialists would have charged because of a lack of experience, competence, or a hidden agenda. Price is only an issue in the absence of true value.

So to the consumer I would say: Don't be cheap. If you're going to be a cheapskate, you're not going to get the best people to represent you. Do you deserve the best representation possible? It's unreasonable to say, "I want you to represent me. I want you to solve my problems.

If you're not willing to pay for the best, then you deserve to get discount service.

I want you to help me become fulfilled as a person and lead me to financial freedom so I can fulfill myself in every way," and then say, "Oh by the way, I don't want to pay you what you're worth." If you're not willing to pay for the best, then you deserve to get discount service. You're not going to get the same level of service and the same level of performance, but you're going to save a few bucks in the short term. If you're cheap, you're not going to get the expert representation you need.

There are some professionals, of course, who are absolutely inept and who still charge as much as truly brilliant specialists. You can pay huge sums of money to incompetents who are not looking out for your best interests. To avoid these types of so-called "advisors" and to learn how to select superior personnel, please review the section of this book on selecting advisors.

In a world where nearly everything is being discounted or turned into a commodity, determining value is more difficult than ever before. If you surf the web, you will find all kinds of free offers. "Free" software to help you do your own tax returns is available by subscribing to a certain magazine for a year. If you subscribe for two years, you also receive an added bonus: software that will help you write your own living trust. "Free" investment advice is everywhere. Do you really believe in such a thing as *excellent* free advice or service? How can anything of great value actually be free? From time to time, you will come across some reasonably valuable free items or services, but nothing great comes easily or for free. Often this is a cruel lesson of life. Let's hope you've already learned it.

Top-notch professionals utilize many different methods of billing or compensation. The method most excellent performers use is a "value billing" system. In essence, value billing has little to do with the time spent (hourly rate) and more to do with achieving the objective. Like in the story of the retired plant supervisor, you are charged for the depth, breadth and wisdom that comes through relevant experience to deliver the desired result.

The best advice I can offer is this: In order to develop truly great outcomes, you must think and act in a win-win paradigm. To get what you want, you must help others get what they want. It must be fair for everyone, not just great for you. If you do not embrace this new paradigm of outcome-based value billing, then you must recognize that someone is losing. Anything less than a win-win situation equals a zero sum game in which only one party in the relationship receives true value.

Here's the most astounding part of this win-win paradigm: Great people produce great outcomes, and they *cost* less than people who quote or charge lower prices. Often the price of greatness is higher, but the overall cost is almost always less. I have learned that I get what I want when I make sure everyone involved sees the venture as personally rewarding monetarily, and enjoys the work and the environment. Everyone gets paid well and has fun. Thus, everyone involved wins. What's more, they will be available and dedicated the next time I need their assistance.

Life is a team event. Success demands a great team comprised of all-stars. All-stars won't work if they aren't getting paid enough or if it isn't fun, because they don't have to work on unrewarding cases or with unpleasant or uncooperative people.

A few years ago, I received a phone call from a stockbroker who had been referred to me by his firm's management. He demanded that I come to Alaska in February to meet with one of his potential clients. I politely declined. He complained to his managers, who apparently felt I was arrogant because I had rejected this so-called "opportunity." "Don't you realize this broker is one of our largest producers?" they asked. "Most people would jump at the chance to work with him."

I gently explained that what was perceived as an opportunity by the broker was not an attractive expenditure of the time, talent and resources of my firm. In our initial phone conversation, the broker had said, "I just prospected a guy who's worth over $50 million. I think I can drag him into a meeting with you." My response had been, "I appreciate your confidence in my firm. However, before we meet with someone, it is important that they read my book or watch our video and pay for the initial meeting. Why don't we have the initial interview over the telephone and save your client thousands of dollars in time and travel expense? The phone interview will give everyone the opportunity to decide whether or not we should work together." The broker was shocked that I wasn't ready to hop on the next flight to Alaska (in February!) and astounded that my firm had certain requirements that must be met before a meeting was scheduled.

The broker was suffering from a type of business-culture clash. In his environment, someone would have to be nuts not to travel far and wide to meet face-to-face with someone worth $50 million. However, in our value-based culture at EFS, we see it differently.

In order to make the most of everyone's time, talents and resources, we have developed a system that enables us to meet only with truly interested and qualified potential clients. By reading my book or watching our video, potential strategic planning clients can determine if they like our philosophy or not. A few hundred dollars for a telephone conference is a small price to pay for a due-diligence interview to see if they like our process. It also allows my company to determine A.) if we can provide value to them, and B.) if it will be a pleasant and financially rewarding endeavor for all involved.

In the EFS culture, we don't sell financial products to consumers because we want to remain unbiased, third-party advisors with no hidden agendas. We have no salespeople because we receive a consistent flow of pre-qualified, motivated client referrals from satisfied clients and other advisors. We are not salespeople who run here and there to chase prospective clients. Our behavior is consistent with our mission to educate and empower; therefore, we provide books, videos, audiotapes, training and consulting to help people identify and achieve their goals. It is really quite simple. EFS seeks to:

- Help the client achieve a better vision of who they are and what they really want to accomplish.

- Educate clients and other advisors.

- Empower clients and other advisors.

- Provide articulate macro and micro strategic plans which accurately describe and fulfill the clients' desired outcomes.

- Facilitate outcomes in which everyone who should be or needs to be involved wins.

Some financial services firms have begun to see our system as a superior method of engaging in business. Neither the broker in Alaska nor his manager appreciated our culture. They did not have a win-win, value-based paradigm. They live in a world where chasing clients is the norm.

When you are good enough to capture and dominate a market niche, you cannot deviate from your system to satisfy those who won't even try to understand better methods. EFS was recently approached by a financial advisor with a firm we had only recently begun working with. When this advisor learned of EFS' client engagement process, he was surprised and pointed out that "every financial advisor, attorney and accountant in this country would buy my potential clients lunch or dinner at the best restaurant around just to meet them."

I suggested he tell his clients that and then share our client engagement process with them. He tried it. The outcome was as we expected and as it usually is. After all, would you want to use a neurosurgeon who bought you dinner just to make a sales pitch?

Fifteen minutes into the meeting, these now highly qualified prospective clients indicated that not only did they want to engage EFS, they wanted to make sure we developed a win-win format for everyone involved. Later the financial advisor turned to us and said, "That's the first time ever in my career that a client's concern over my compensation was a positive. Most people try to negotiate my compensation down to nothing. This is going to be better for everyone." Unlike the broker in Alaska and his manager, this advisor was able to see the world through a different set of lenses. He now lives a better paradigm, and is more powerful and effective personally and for his clients.

The truth is that great people produce great outcomes. It is best if everyone has a financial stake in the desired outcome. Sales systems are unnecessary in this type of work. Client fulfillment systems and value-based, outcome-driven billing is the best way to deliver and receive great performance.

Enduring Value

Commodities and transactions are easily found on price lists. True value —the kind that exists and endures beyond the boundaries of "the deal"— is somewhat ambiguous and thus cannot be printed on some generic list of services or transactions. Integrity, technical competency, relevant experience and creativity combined with wisdom are the professional values for which intelligent, successful clients hunger. True value is often a subtle thing, best determined by each project or desired outcome. The wisest clients know that their best outcomes will be achieved through competent, caring, creative vision, sound execution and the principle of win/win for everyone involved.

When I want an important project accomplished brilliantly, I find the very best professionals and compensate them so that they have a stake in the endeavor. Great people are hard to find and are worth their weight in gold. They do not work off of a price list. They are not commodities. Great professionals produce results of enduring value.

Bruce R. Wright, 1997

V

Wealth: How to Use It

33

Creating, Living and Leaving a Legacy

What is life all about? This is one of the questions along with "Who am I?" and "Why am I here?" that have perplexed mankind from the beginning. What purpose does your life serve? Or in other words, what is your mission? What is truly important to you? What inspires you, or perhaps, what really makes you angry, and what are you doing about it?

With well-structured and intelligently managed wealth comes the freedom to pursue what we really want to do with our lives. I believe wealth gives us the unique opportunity to create a legacy. If we're not engaged in some type of mission, we're not going to be happy. We're not going to be fulfilled. Imagine yourself at your own funeral. What will you be remembered for? How do you define success? How do you really achieve fulfillment? One universal truth is that fulfillment comes from being of value and offering service to other people or to viable, worthwhile causes, purposes and missions. Your 100-year plan can help you create and carry out your life-fulfilling legacy.

Here are three ways you can make a difference:

- You can dedicate your time to a cause.

- You can finance a mission or a cause.

- You can provide an example to influence other people to subscribe to your values or to support your mission or cause.

I think most people do not consider that they have a mission. I believe that's why a lot of people are not really as happy as they could be. I also believe that you achieve a greater level of fulfillment when you're working on something bigger than yourself, and what you're working on is about more than just making money. I cannot convey this message adequately to everyone. Not everyone is ready to hear it or act upon it. How does one motivate people to reach for a higher purpose in their lives?

Everything in your life could be going well. Your investment advisors could be doing a fantastic job. Your wealth may be performing. You're successful. Everything is going marvelously, yet still, you may not be truly happy. Well, why are you not truly happy? You need to take a look at the list of objectives you have written down. When you answered the goal-setting questions, were there philosophical and emotional things you would like to have accomplished? Were there people or causes you wanted to help? Was there something in the world you wanted to change? Maybe all of your financial objectives are being met, but the problem is complacency. If you have no mission, cause or purpose, you start to realize there is a void. We're not going to be happy unless we meet certain criteria in our lives that go beyond our personal needs for food, shelter, clothing, travel, hobbies, etc. It gets into the fundamental issues of the human spirit, the need to be involved in something bigger than ourselves, the need to know we left a mark on the world, the need to know that our life mattered. We need to know that we are leaving a legacy.

You may be worth $30 million or $3 million, or perhaps even $300,000, and what used to be important to you is not enough anymore. If you're in the construction business, going out and building houses may not be important to you anymore. I'm not saying building houses is unimportant work. I'm saying that the talents and skills that made you successful enough to be worth millions may be stagnating now. You have to ask yourself: How much is enough? And when is it enough? If you really only need $200,000 of net annual income to live comfortably and you've got millions of dollars in resources, perhaps what you need to do is refocus your life and direct those talents, abilities, skills and interests toward something with greater meaning than building houses. If you stop building houses, the person who buys your company will continue to build houses. If your company goes out of existence, someone else will continue to build houses. There will always be somebody around to build houses. However, there are never enough talented, competent people available to champion viable, intelligent causes.

I was discussing a financial advisor's goals with him, and he said his objective was to become proficient enough in his job that he had more time to spend with his wife and children. He also wanted to be able to spend a couple of hours a week helping to coach young people at the Boys & Girls Club in entrepreneurship and how to get out of their present circumstances and make something of themselves. It hit him in a profound way once we started working together that whereas he used to work just to make money, now he was working toward achieving financial independence. Eventually, he was now confident, he would have the power to spend his time—as much time as he wanted to, two hours a week, two hours a day, 20 hours a day if he wanted to—with his family and helping young people achieve more. This would give his life far more meaning than managing people's investment portfolios.

So, what is it that is going to make you happy? Is it helping blind children get seeing eye dogs, providing wheelchairs for people who can't afford them, helping abused kids? Is it teaching entrepreneurial skills to inner-city youth? Protecting endangered whales? What is going to make you feel fulfilled? What is your cause? Your mission? Your purpose? What is your legacy going to be? You have an opportunity to create a legacy for yourself and benefit something bigger than yourself by selecting a cause or causes that you want to support. You need to include this mission in your goals and agenda, and implement strategies that will ensure that your desires will be carried out.

How important is money? If you really want to make a difference, how is your money going to make a difference? If it's sitting around doing little or nothing for you, if it's not producing as much growth or income as it should, and if it's sitting in a position where the government will just confiscate 55% of it, how effective is that?

If you have all these blessings, all these talents, all these advantages, and your choice is to sit back and do less than you are capable of when you could make a substantial difference, then you have to live or die with that decision.

What if you could have done more, you could have been better, you could have lengthened your stride, you could have made a positive difference in the lives of many people, but you didn't? Instead, you got comfortable. You got near the top of your mountain and you sat there and said, "Oh, this is nice. I'll just camp here and enjoy myself from now on." In effect, you retired from the game. You gave up. You quit climbing.

So who loses? Well, you lose a whole bunch of money to the government by default. But more important, all the things you could have done, would have done, should have done, don't happen because you quit, because you didn't act as a good steward over what you had. To many people, this is a spiritual issue. I know from experience that people who pursue a proactive course will find it difficult and challenging. However, the rewards in terms of personal fulfillment are tremendous. Unless you play this game, unless you participate in this battle, you're not going to be fulfilled. You're going to know down deep inside that you could have, would have, should have done something better—and you didn't do it.

Some people don't do it because they are lazy. It may also be that they are too comfortable, too engulfed in fear, or just too uninformed. Worst of all, some people think they are the center of the universe, thus failing to see the opportunities available to be proactively engaged in helping others. I hope this won't be the case for you, for myself or for our children.

Earlier I mentioned a client who plans to charter a Concorde jet on New Year's Eve for the year 2000. Does it make him selfish because he could be spending that money on medical treatment for needy children? No. If you believed in that philosophy, then you would have to live in a hovel. You'd have to wear rags. You'd have to take all of your resources and give them to other people. If in fact you did that, you would be less effective. You wouldn't be able to accumulate $20 million in net worth. We need to spend enough money on ourselves to alleviate our personal concerns and fears so that we're more effective in helping other people.

Let's say you are spending $200,000 a year on yourself and giving $100,000 to charity, and you learn that you could A.) have even more safety in your investments, B.) still have $200,000 net to spend on yourself, and C.) have $300,000 instead of $100,000 to fund your mission. Could you be happy staying in your existing position? If you were just giving away the $300,000 to any charity who happened to ask, then you might not feel very fulfilled. But if you felt that you were making a difference, supporting a cause you truly believed in, that's where many find happiness.

Just the mere act of giving away money is not where happiness comes from. It's not enough. There may be a sense of relief in it. You may feel that in essence you have "bought" some degree of salvation or fulfillment. The experience of giving is the reward. But there is a difference between charitable giving and funding a mission. If you have a mission to support, you won't miss the money.

I met a lady through her stockbroker who was giving away $100,000 a year and was perfectly happy with that. She was worth several million. Now her investment advisor had told her that although she thought she was making "safe" investments, she was actually losing a half of a percent on her money every year to taxes and inflation. (Remember the discussion in Chapter Six about the internal rate of return on your entire net worth?)

We proposed several strategies and tactics, including some charitable options, that would allow her to protect her principal, increase her income and reduce her taxes. By restructuring her wealth, she would be able to do all the things she used to do; in addition, she could use $300,000 to fund her mission instead of only $100,000. She had asked herself the questions we've discussed about philosophical and emotional goals. Was there something she would like to change in the world? Was there a cause she would like to support? There was. She wanted to leave a legacy of supporting education and protecting the U.S. Constitution.

By improving this woman's tactical position, we empowered her to further her goals and objectives. At the same time, we reduced the fear in her life. She's less fearful because she's more diversified, more knowledgeable and more in control. Because she's better informed and took action, she's more protected. We increased her happiness because now she can do more of what she wants to do. She can fund her mission; she can create and *live* her legacy. With proper planning and action, so can you.

34

Children and Charity (First, Do No Harm)

How much money should we leave to our children or heirs? Most people would answer that question by saying, "All of it. We should give everything we can to our children." My answer is: not necessarily.

Suppose one of your goals is to provide for your children and make them financially independent, and you determine that based on today's dollars your kids would be financially independent if they each had $7 million in assets working for them. If you have a large enough estate to give each of them $50 million, should you? That becomes a moral issue. Do they really need $50 million? Would giving them $50 million hurt them or destroy them in a moral sense? Would they become lazy? Would they become spoiled? Would they become arrogant? Or would they be able to put that money to good use?

My feeling is that we don't know what our kids or grandchildren are going to do. One option is to make the kids financially independent to whatever extent you want to, if at all, and direct the rest of the money into a private family foundation or supporting organization which carries out your goals and objectives philanthropically. By having your heirs, your children, grandchildren and even great-grandchildren interact with such a private foundation or supporting organization, you give them the opportunity to carry out or carry on the belief system that has helped to make your family (and perhaps the country) successful. But if you just give your heirs a whole bunch of money and say, "Here's all the money you could possibly ever want," and they don't have the necessary discipline or understanding to manage their lives or their money wisely, they'll probably lose, or worse, abuse that money. They could spend it on sports cars or drugs or on behavior you would never approve of. You could, in effect, become the sponsor of behavior you vehemently disagree with.

The most important rule when providing an inheritance to family, friends or charity is this: *Do not hurt those people or causes you love.* Far too often, people are damaged through the laws of unintended consequences. The best gifts we can make are those that lift others. Carelessness on the part of generous people frequently results in the opposite of the desired outcome. Money doesn't always make everything better. Sometimes it just exacerbates problems. We must consider the stewardship abilities of those people and/or charities we desire to help. Intelligent love, sometimes even tough love, is necessary to avoid the "killing with kindness" that comes as a result of right-brain dominant compassion or incomplete and inaccurate thinking, planning and action.

I think this is a problem a lot of people have as they look at their wealth. Many people have a tendency not to look hard enough at the issues. Sometimes they just don't have all of the facts and can't make well thought out decisions because they lack information. If we put these things in perspective, we're trying to employ a systematic approach to our wealth that carries out all of our philosophical needs and supports our 100-year plan.

If one of your goals is to benefit your causes, are you willing to sacrifice that goal so that your heirs will receive an extra $200,000 or $300,000 beyond what they really need? We have to ask ourselves, "How much is enough?," for our heirs as well as for ourselves.

One of my strategies is to avoid taxes. Suppose that 20 years from now all of my children are grown and three of them are very successful in business—so successful, in fact, that the inheritance I have left them isn't helping their financial situation or improving their quality of life. Instead, it is increasing their taxes and contradicting my goals and objectives with respect to money going to Congress. In other words, if my children have a net worth of $10 million apiece, giving each of them another $10 million isn't going to improve their lifestyle. All it's going to do is create an additional $10 million of estate, which would then be $20 million, and the government would want to take 55% of it when they die. So if my objective is to not give Congress an inheritance, it may not make any sense whatsoever for me to increase the inheritance to my children above and beyond what they've been able to accumulate on their own.

It is not necessarily a charity *versus* children scenario either. As the title of this chapter states, it's a matter of children *and* charity. Perhaps the best way to look at it is this: How can you help your children *and* involve them in your legacy and your values for multiple generations? If you believe that you, your heirs, your community or your causes can do a better job with your hard-earned wealth than Congress, you need to take action now. Don't lose it by default through procrastination.

The discovery, creation, building and funding of a legacy is a complex arena. Once people decide to explore this subject, they will find no shortage of advisors ready to offer all kinds of help. You must apply what you've read in earlier chapters regarding hidden agendas, smiling crocodiles and selecting the right advisors. Failure to make the right decisions in this important area can have far-reaching effects on your heirs, your legacy and your peace of mind.

35

Sweet Charity:
How to Choose or Create a Charity
to Efficiently Fulfill
Your Mission or Legacy

Once you determine which cause or causes you wish to support as part of your mission, you can begin to explore charitable options. A private foundation or supporting organization may be the answer for you, or you may choose to support established public charitable organizations. There are many good, deserving charitable organizations, but there are organizations to be wary of. In addition to meeting with or touring the facilities of the charities, I counsel clients to request and examine the current business plan, mission statements and the last three years' financial statements of the charities they are interested in. Along with your advisory team, you will want to make sure the charitable institutions fulfill the objectives set forth as part of your 100-year plan.

You also want to make sure the charitable organizations you're interested in have a sound plan for dealing with the problem you're interested in. There are some people who are not cautious enough in selecting charities.

For example, there may be two charities working to eliminate drunk driving. One charity pushes for vehicle regulation. They want to restrict the size of gas tanks so that a car can only go 100 miles on a tank of gas instead of 400 miles, the reasoning being that a car is four times more

Be sure the charity you support has a sound plan for dealing with the problem you're interested in. Some people are not cautious enough in selecting charities.

likely to be involved in a drunk driving incident if it can go four times as far. Naturally the charity will have scientific analysis to support this absurd position. The other charity wants to target the drunk driver as the person responsible for drunk driving accidents.

Obviously the second group is going to be more productive in reducing drunk driving because it goes to the root of the problem, the drunk driver. We need to select charities that take a sound approach to achieving the desired outcome.

A great deal of time, energy, talent and money are often wasted on illogical and ineffective approaches. We must be especially leery of causes promoted with highly political or emotional rhetoric. Generally speaking, the more emotional the plea, the less substance and more distortions of fact you will find. You must be thorough and courageous in pursuing a truly effective mission. You will need to balance both the left-brain (analytical) and right-brain (emotional) issues. It's best to select charities that offer pragmatic, result-oriented programs to support what is for you an important emotional or philosophical cause. A wise person focuses on core issues, not the symptoms or emotional diatribe or hype. What makes this so difficult is that the most effective approaches aren't always popular or politically correct.

Just as in selecting advisors, being able to recognize others' agendas comes into play when selecting charities. You need to make sure a charitable organization's agenda is in harmony with yours. For example, if you were to create a charitable remainder trust, you might be concerned with achieving the following:

- Maintaining control over assets and decisions

- Maximizing income for you during your lifetime

- Maximizing tax benefits to you and your heirs

- Redirecting would-be tax dollars to causes that truly fulfill your mission

- Creating a plan that looks at the big picture, your lifetime and legacy goals in your 100-year plan, and inheritance for your heirs

The agenda for the charitable institution (remainderman beneficiaries) may in many important ways differ from your agenda. For example, some charities may have no interest in examining your 100-year plan. They may, in fact, be more interested in the following than they are in achieving your agenda:

- Paying as little income to you as possible

- Controlling assets directly by acting as trustee or indirectly through a third-party trustee with whom they have a close relationship

- Securing as much of the trust as possible for themselves instead of dividing it with other charities you may be interested in

Consider these objectives, and it's easy to recognize different agendas. Often, would-be trustors (clients/donors) want higher income levels than the charity would like to see distributed. After all, if the trust pays you less income, the trust assets eventually passing to charity may be greater. Also, some charities or their representatives may have a limited perspective and/or don't know how to consider the big picture. They often lack the technical ability and knowledge to answer potential donors' questions accurately and fully or address *all* of your concerns. This becomes particularly evident when an expert advisor is brought in by the potential donor.

As much as I hate to say it, some charities are simply out to rip you off and won't tell you the truth or at best will only tell you part of the truth to accomplish their goals. So choose charities carefully or consider creating your own charity or private foundation.

In order to gain more insight into the issues of philanthropy, I refer you to *The Wright Revolution in Philanthropy*, a guide I wrote to help consumers and charities create win/win relationships. It is also helpful for advisors wishing to gain greater insight to benefit their clients, and to charitable board members eager to fully endow the charities they serve. In fact, anyone involved in charitable remainder trusts, gift annuities, the establishment of supporting organizations, private family foundations and the like will consider it a must-read before implementation to avoid regrettable situations later.

36

The Truth Will Set You Free

There are many truths in this book which, when properly applied, can help you achieve greater wealth, happiness and freedom. Now it's up to you to recognize and use these truths. Remember the old saying, "The truth hurts"? My experience is that the truth can be painful; but it's only painful when our actions are not in harmony with the truth.

By reading this book, you've shown that you at least want to pursue the truth. Some people really don't want to learn the truth. They really don't want their paradigms and perceptions challenged. And some people have the attitude that truth doesn't exist, everything is relative and it's people's perceptions that really matter.

When I hear that statement, I can't let it go unchallenged, for there are definite truths in this world. Let me share with you a little debate. Jean says to Adam, "There is no such thing as truth. One person's truth is not necessarily another person's truth. If you really believe something hard enough, then that becomes your truth. It's all relative. Perception is, in fact, reality."

Adam disagrees and says, "An individual's perception of reality is not necessarily accurate or true. If a person has a misguided perception of reality, that person is likely to be injured or perhaps injure others as a result of the incorrect or inaccurate perception. If you don't believe me, come with me to the top of a 20-story building."

Jean doesn't agree and goes with Adam to the building. As the two are standing on the roof, Adam, who believes that there are absolute truths, asks, "What would happen if I dropped a soda pop can from this roof?"

Jean responds, "It would fall."

"If I dropped it 10 times in a row," Adam asks, "how many times would it fall? If I dropped it 1,000 times, how many times would it fall?"

"Every time," answers Jean.

Adam then says, "Gravity is an example of a truth. A person's perception of gravity has little to do with the way gravity actually works. At least here on earth, gravity works the same way every time for everyone. Regardless of anybody's perception of the issue, that soda can will fall 100% of the time."

Jean is still not convinced and says, "Well, you aren't taking into account the fact that people, unlike soda cans, have attitudes. Attitudes and perceptions are crucially important. In fact, attitude is practically everything."

Adam, believing in absolute truths, says, "A person's attitude with regard to truths is irrelevant," and leads Jean to the edge of the roof.

Adam says, "If you have the most positive mental attitude in the world, and you really, truly believe that gravity won't affect you, then I would suggest that you look over the edge. That's a mighty long drop down there. Since I believe in gravity, and my perception of gravity is in line with reality, I'm not going to step off the building."

Adam continues, "If you still believe that gravity won't have an effect on you because of your attitude and perception, then hang one foot off the edge of the roof. As soon as you remove your second foot from the edge of the building, you're going to experience the reality of gravity firsthand. In a relatively short period of time, you will receive a crash course in the effects of absolute truths. You will see that a misguided perception can be very harmful to an individual or to those individuals with whom you interact."

The point, of course, is that gravity is a law which applies to all objects here upon the earth. The effects of gravity are somewhat different on Mars, and different again on Pluto; I suppose in other universes the difference is greater still. But here in *this* universe, on *this* planet, there's a certain way gravity works. It's a truth. Your perception of gravity, if it is not in harmony with truth, can get you killed. Just because you think something is a certain way doesn't make it so.

People have different approaches to the truth. Truth is like a bull's-eye target. The truth is the center of the bull's eye. There are some people who will be right in the center of the target, who know there is such a thing as truth, can recognize the truth and will go right toward it.

There are other people who will acknowledge that truth exists, but because of preconceived notions, prejudice, incomplete information or inaccurate paradigms cannot deal directly with the truth. Maybe they'll get in the outer ring that's near the truth, but they never actually reach the truth.

Then there are other people who are so far away from the truth that they're not even on the target. They don't acknowledge that truth exists or that they should be trying to reach it.

One of the big paradigm challenges in this life is that we have to adapt ourselves to the truth rather than wait for the truth to adapt to our paradigms or to us. The truth has no respect for individual paradigms, just as gravity has no respect for individuals' perceptions, attitudes or beliefs. If you want to break free of gravity and fly, you have to consider the effect of gravity and incorporate it into your plans.

This concept of truth is relevant with regard to financial situations. A direct correlation to gravity in a financial sense could be rising interest rates. You may think rising interest rates won't hurt you; that's your perception. But if your investments are positioned in certain markets that are sensitive to interest rate increases, you could lose a lot of money. It doesn't matter what you believe, the market's always right. The market does what it does regardless of how you want it to be. Your perception of the market, whether it's the bond market, stock market, real estate market, interest rates, inflation, your own business field or profession, is relevant in that you'll be successful or unsuccessful based upon how accurate your perceptions are, how aligned with reality they are. And perhaps even more important than that, your success will be determined by what actions you take or fail to take.

In order to be successful, we must do the following:

1. Recognize that the truth exists
2. Recognize the importance of the truth
3. Realize that our perceptions may be out of line with the truth
4. Make an effort to find the truth
5. Recognize the truth when we find it
6. Adapt our perceptions to match the truth
7. Act upon the truth

It's not enough just to look for truth. It's not enough to go the next step and recognize it when you find it. The greatest difficulty or pain comes when we have to change ourselves so our actions are in harmony with the truth.

I honestly believe that everyone would benefit by adopting a 100-year philosophy of life. Not everyone (consumer or advisor) is capable of thinking in macro, visionary terms. If one cannot *think* macro, then one cannot *do* macro. Those who cannot think or do in macro terms obviously cannot "become elephants" themselves or help anyone else become an elephant. I'm convinced that while everyone could benefit from macro strategic planning, some people just aren't interested.

It works like this: On a benefit or needs scale where 0 equals no need and 5 equals immediate or urgent need, everyone would rate at level 4 or 5.

Benefit/Needs Assessment

0	5

We must remember that old saying, "You can lead a horse to water but you can't make it drink." Of course, it helps if you start with a thirsty horse. On the same kind of scale, you could rate people's interest, or thirst, like this:

Thirstometer

0	5

***A horse won't drink until it's thirsty; people won't
hear the truth until they're ready.***

People have varying degrees of thirst. Some rate at level
0, or no interest, while others rate at level 5. There is little
if any correspondence between need and thirst. Over time,
some horses get exercised and become thirsty enough to
drink. For some people it takes a major crisis to move them
to act. If your spouse or business partner isn't "thirsty"
enough to do what's best, don't despair. Perhaps you'll just
need to exercise them a bit to get them thirsty. Perhaps there
is a hidden crisis about to shake things up and they just don't
know about it yet. Don't give up on getting the "perfect" or
better calendar and higher quality of life you deserve. If you
behave in an intelligently proactive manner (no nagging!),
eventually you can exercise even the most stubborn mules
enough to get them thirsty.

A philosopher once said, "A mind stretched to a new di-
mension never returns to its original form." Although there
may be growing pains, I have never seen an increase in knowledge and perspective hurt anyone in the long run. It is my
hope that, in the limited space of this book, I have provided
you with helpful knowledge, taught you a few truths and
perhaps given you a new perspective which will enable you
to set wonderful goals, reach your goals, achieve your higher
purpose and live a more effective, happy, fulfilling life.

Are you ready to develop your goals, your 100-year plan,
and begin living your "perfect calendar"? The greatest part
of your life is waiting to happen. The only thing it is waiting for is you!

Have a great life!

About the Author

Bruce R. Wright is the founder and chairman of The Wright Company. For more than a decade, America's leading financial organizations, elite professionals and their clients have benefited from Wright's innovative Macro Strategic Planning approach to understanding and managing related financial issues. Since neither Wright nor any of his companies are involved in the sale or promotion of investment or insurance products, his insight is highly valued for his impartial "outside the box" focus.

A noted advisor, educator, speaker and author, Wright is revolutionizing the financial services industry by providing dynamic, leading-edge systems, tools, and techniques that help both professionals and consumers alike reach their financial goals and live the calendar of their dreams.